My Product Management Toolkit

Tools and Techniques to Become an Outstanding Product Manager

Marc Abraham

ISBN: 1984007319
ISBN-13: 9781984007315
Library of Congress Control Number: 2018901700
CreateSpace Independent Publishing Platform, North Charleston, SC

To my amazing family, Tracy, Oscar, and Zac

Contents

Introduction

Why This Book?

Over the past few years, many people have asked me for practical advice about product management. Take Stephen, for example, founder of an early-stage start-up who wanted to know how to conduct customer research on a shoestring budget. Or Rita, who had been a product manager for only a short while and asked me about how to best create and drive a product vision.

People like Stephen and Rita inspired me to write down my own lessons learned and the tools I used as a product manager. I published my first blog post, titled "My Product Management Toolkit," in January 2016, and I wrote about how to best create a product vision.[1] The feedback I received from fellow product managers spurred me on to write many more "toolkit" posts, and I have published more than twenty of these as of the time of writing.[2]

The number of views, the quality of the feedback I received, and the range of people saying, "You should write a book," encouraged me to collate some of my favourite product management tools and techniques and to gather them together in print (or pixels, depending on how you're reading this). This book is by no means a substitute for some of the great product management books already out there.[3] If anything, I hope you will find this book to be a useful supplement, focussing on practical tools to assist you in your day-to-day life as a product manager and helping you to create great products.

---

[1] "My Product Management Toolkit (1)—Product Vision," Marc Abraham, January 8, 2016, https://marcabraham.com/2016/01/08/my-product-management-toolkit-1-product-vision/.

[2] "My Product Management Toolkit (25): Understanding the 'Unit Economics' of Your Product," Marc Abraham, December 28, 2017, https://marcabraham.com/2017/12/28/my-product-management-toolkit-25-understanding-the-unit-economics-of-your-product/.

[3] I highly recommend the following product management books: Marty Cagan, *Inspired: How to Create Products Customers Love* (San Francisco: SVPG Press, 2008); Eric Ries, *The Lean Startup: How Today's Entrepreneurs Use Continuous Innovation to Create Radically Successful Businesses* (New York: Crown Business, 2011); Jeff Gothelf and Josh Seiden, *Lean UX: Designing Great Products with Agile Teams* (Sebastopol, CA: O'Reilly Media, 2016); Roman Pichler, *Strategize: Product Strategy and Product Roadmap Practices for the Digital Age* (Hempstead, United Kingdom: Pichler Consulting, 2016); Richard Banfield, Martin Eriksson, and Nate Walkingshaw, *Product Leadership: How Top Product Managers Launch Awesome Products and Build Successful Teams* (Sebastopol, CA: O'Reilly Media, 2017).

I have a final disclaimer before you carry on reading: this book is not meant to be the definitive list of all the answers or tools you can use when creating products. In fact, it is quite the opposite. Please treat the suggested tools, techniques, and approaches as you see fit. For avoidance of doubt, I use tools, approaches, and techniques interchangeably, and together they make up my armoury as a product manager. It is important to acknowledge that every product or product organisation is unique and requires its own individual approach and that the tools and techniques you will use are likely to vary, depending on your situation or challenge.

My hope is that from reading this book, you will find at least one tool or technique that you will be able to apply to your product immediately and perhaps some remaining tools to add to your long-term toolkit. Equally, I would love to hear from you about any successful tools or techniques that I might have missed in this book so that I can, in turn, add them to my own product management toolkit!

Who Is This Book For?

Naturally, I would like every reader to find this book valuable. However, I am deliberately concentrating on some of the more tactical aspects of product management so that product managers with one to two years of experience can broaden their toolkits in order to become outstanding.

In addition to tactical tools and techniques, I will also introduce some of the more strategic aspects of product management, such as defining a product vision and creating shared product goals. Whether you are a first-time product manager or a fifteen-year product veteran, it is important to understand the basics of (product) strategy, especially as you are getting started with managing a product. Experience has taught me that thinking strategically helps you to build the right product right for the right reasons and for the right rationale.

My hope is that you will revert to this book as and when you need it, finding within it a tool you can use for the opportunity or challenge at hand.

How Are This Book and Its Chapters Structured?

The book is structured in such a way that it starts with the very foundations. In chapters 1 and 2, we will look at what a product is and what makes a (good) product manager, respectively. Once we have looked more inwardly, we will shift our attention outward to the customer. The customer and customer needs are central to chapter 3, in which we will explore how to determine who your customers are and how to best learn from them.

Chapter 4 is all about getting started when managing a product and examining tools and techniques that will help you on your way when either creating a new product or iterating on an existing one. Once we have addressed how to get started, in chapter 5 we will look at the key day-to-day responsibilities when managing a product.

In the final part of this book, chapter 6, we change our focus from products to people and cover some of the tools and techniques key to managing people when developing successful products.

Each chapter has the following basic structure:

- **Goal:** This section outlines the learning outcome for the chapter. For example, "To understand and be able to communicate the foundations of product management" is the goal of the first chapter of this book.
- **Related tools and techniques to consider:** This section includes the specific tactics and approaches that will be covered in the chapter. In chapter 1, for example, we will look at creating a problem statement as a useful technique for determining which problem your product should solve.
- **In-depth look:** The body of the chapter will offer an in-depth view of the relevant tools and techniques as well as their underlying rationales. I will use real-life examples, either my own or others, and lessons learned to illustrate the different aspects of the toolkit.
- **Key takeaways:** This section summarizes each chapter and is followed by practical examples of where and how to best apply the tools and techniques covered in the chapter.
- **How to apply these takeaways:** This section includes several practical examples and tips with regard to applying the key takeaways from each chapter.

1
Hygiene Factors for Every Product Manager

Goal

To understand and be able to communicate the foundations of product management.

Related Tools and Techniques to Consider

- Use the **hammer analogy** to explain the difference between a product and a service.
- Tell a story about **customer value** to explain what makes a product and how product managers constantly operate at the intersection between user experience, business, and technology.
- Write **problem statements** to help you focus on key problems to solve.
- Use product **life cycles,** such as the iPod, to help illustrate the difference between project and product management.

Introduction

One reason product management is such an appealing career is you get to sit at the intersection of technology, business, and design.
—Gayle Laakmann McDowell and Jackie Bavaro, *Cracking the PM Interview*

"So what is it that you do?" is probably one of the most dreaded questions at birthday parties, weddings, or, frankly, anytime you meet someone new socially. How does one explain in a few sentences the role of a product manager? There are so many things that you are as a product manager, and at the same time, there are so many things that you are not. Where does one start?

In this first chapter, we will look at the fundamentals of product management. What is a product? What is product management, and how is it different from project management? In this chapter, we will explore definitions and concepts that underpin product management.

1. What Is a Product?

When I am asked, "So what is that do you do?" I typically start with a brief definition of what a product is and then mention the type of product(s) that I work on. I have learned to adapt the meaning of the word *product* as provided by the dictionary:[4]

- An article or substance that is manufactured or refined for sale.
- A thing or person that is the result of an action or process.
- A quantity obtained by multiplying quantities together, or from an analogous algebraic operation.

I struggle with these definitions because most of the products I have worked on feel very far removed from any of these dictionary explanations. Having worked on, among others, mobile apps, websites, APIs, online marketplaces, and streaming services, I find it difficult to reconcile these products with the standard definitions. However, this does not make the dictionary definitions obsolete. If anything, it shows that managing digital products is still a relatively new discipline. As a result, it can be challenging to explain *within* the technology space what a product manager does, let alone to people I meet who don't work in technology.

When explaining what it is that I do, I therefore try to keep it straightforward and explain that product management relates to both physical and nonphysical (i.e., digital) products, given that one could be building cars or websites. The question then arises whether a service also counts as a product. Patrick Quattlebaum and Jamin Hegeman, two experienced design directors, use an analogy to explain the difference between products and services: "A product is a hammer, and a service is someone holding the hammer and hammering for you."[5]

- A *product* is a tangible output, which can be measured and counted.
- A *service* is an intangible benefit, which can be related to a product.

---

[4] "Product," *English Oxford Living Dictionaries*, accessed February 3, 2018, https://en.oxforddictionaries.com/definition/product.

[5] "The Difference Between a Product and a Service—as Told with Hammers," Erik Flowers, December 3, 2015, http://www.helloerik.com/the-difference-between-a-product-and-a-service-as-told-with-hammers.

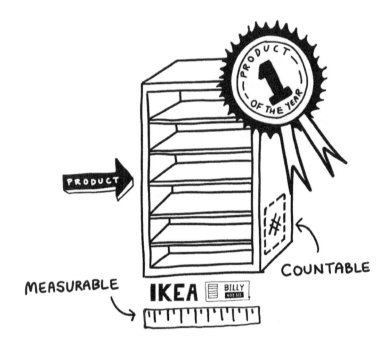

Figure 1.1. IKEA's iconic Billy bookcase is a good example of a product.

Returning to the previous explanation by Quattlebaum and Hegeman, a hammer is a product, and you call it a service when you are actually using a hammer. In the same vein, Billy, IKEA's iconic bookcase, is a good example of a product as a tangible output (fig. 1.1.).

Recently, IKEA acquired TaskRabbit, an on-demand platform for, among other things, hiring people to assemble your Billy bookcase for you.[6] TaskRabbit thus offers a service to customers who have bought a Billy bookcase. (See fig. 1.2.)

---

[6] "IKEA Has Bought TaskRabbit," Megan Rose Dickey, TechCrunch, September 28, 2017, https://techcrunch.com/2017/09/28/ikea-buys-taskrabbit/.

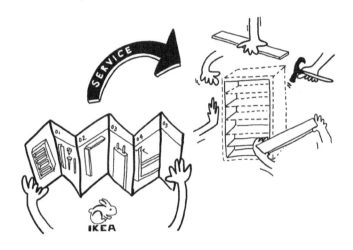

Figure 1.2. Using the TaskRabbit service to assemble an IKEA Billy bookcase

2. Can Digital Products Be Considered Products?

How does the previous explanation of what a product is apply to digital products? For example, as a product manager, I have never worked on cars or juicers. In contrast, my products have always been of a digital nature, be it a web or mobile app.

Does this mean that my products aren't products in the truest sense of the word? Quite the opposite. Roman Pichler, a well-known product management consultant, verbalises this well: "If an asset does not create value for its customers and users for the company, then I don't regard it as a product."[7]

In essence, it does not matter whether a product is digital or physical; it needs to provide value to its users. When referring to products in this book, the term

---

[7] "What Is a Digital Product?," Roman Pichler, June 14, 2016, http://www.romanpichler.com/blog/what-is-a-digital-product/.

product will refer to both physical and digital products. Granted, some of the tools and techniques in this book might naturally be a better fit with digital products, and I will highlight wherever this might be the case.

3. The Product as a Collection of Features

A great product isn't just a collection of features. It's how it all works together.
—Marco Arment, founder of Instapaper

It is often the product's features that determine how successful a product is. In essence, a product is a collection of features. Each of these features not only needs to add value to the user, but they also need to work effectively together and offer a great customer experience. Like Marco Arment argues in his quote that opens this section, if a product is just a collection of random features, it is bound to struggle in communicating its full value to its users.

Let's look at an example of a feature that doesn't necessarily add customer value and one that does: the Samsung Galaxy S6 palm screen grab and the Amazon.com wish list, respectively. Often a product will be made up of several features or components. It is worth noting that not every feature or component adds value to users. For example, I am not convinced of the benefits of using my palms to do screen grabs on the Samsung Galaxy S6 smartphone. This feature feels somewhat counterintuitive and not precise enough. (See fig. 1.3.)

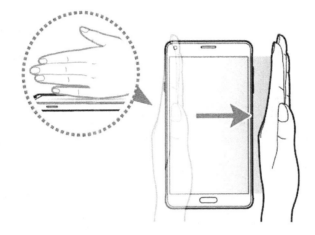

Figure 1.3. Illustration of the screen grab functionality on the Samsung Galaxy S6[8]

In contrast, the wish list feature on Amazon.com really makes it easy for me to keep track of the books I would like to read at some point. It is also an easy place to point other people to for birthday gift ideas. (See fig. 1.4.)

[8] "How to Take Screenshot on Samsung Galaxy S6 and S6 Edge?" Galaxy S6 Guide, accessed February 3, 2018, http://gadgetguideonline.com/galaxys6/samsung-galaxy-s6-guides/how-to-take-screenshot-on-samsung-galaxy-s6-and-s6-edge/.

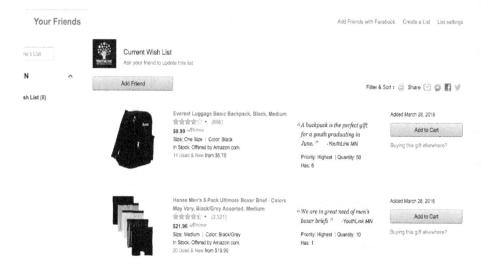

Figure 1.4. Sample Amazon.com wish list[9]

In either case, one could argue that the overall product experience is a good one, irrespective of one or two less effective features. I do believe, however, that the more effective a product's features, the more successful a product is likely to be.

4. What Is Product Management?

"What is product management?" is often treated as the million-dollar question. Product management is a relatively new discipline, and I have found that it means different things to different people and organisations. Looking at products and features in the previous section raises the question of who decides on which features to include in a product. Who makes sure that a product does not become just a bundle of (useless) features? Who manages a product beyond its launch to market?

This is where the role of the product manager comes in. In his book *Inspired: How to Create Products Customers Love*, Marty Cagan talks about the role of the product manager in "discovering a product that is valuable, usable, and feasible."[10]

---

[9] "A Nonprofit Donation Wish List—How Amazon Can Help Your Nonprofit," Chloe Mark, The Nerdy Nonprofit, April 4, 2016, http://www.thenerdynonprofit.com/nonprofit-donation-wish-list/.
[10] Cagan, *Inspired*, vii.

The product manager's ultimate responsibility for defining the solution was one aspect of Cagan's book that struck me the most. Whereas a product manager does bear this responsibility, it is the engineering team and designers who know best what is possible, and they must ultimately implement and deliver the solution.

A friend of mine and a product management veteran, Martin Eriksson, introduced a Venn diagram to go with Cagan's description, outlining how, as a product manager, one operates at the intersection of business, technology, and user experience. (See fig. 1.5.)

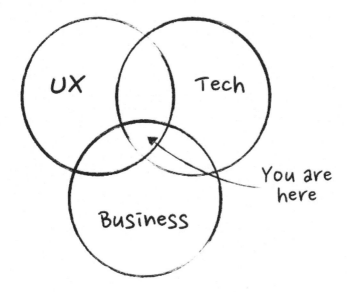

Figure 1.5. Operating at the intersection of business, technology, and user experience[11]

Product management is a critical business function, having to constantly balance the needs of the customer (user experience, or UX) with business interests (business) and technical viability (tech). As product managers, we often work very closely with developers and designers, as well as liaise with business stakeholders and customers, to make sure we create great products that offer both business and customer value.

---

[11] "What, Exactly, Is a Product Manager?" Martin Eriksson, Mind the Product, October 5, 2011, http://www.mindtheproduct.com/2011/10/what-exactly-is-a-product-manager/.

5. Start with the Customers and Their Problem(s)

We are not competitor-obsessed, we are customer-obsessed. We start with what the customer needs and we work backwards.

—Jeff Bezos

It is easy to get excited about a specific product or feature without really addressing whether it solves a problem for our customers and whether this problem is worth solving in the first place. Concentrating up-front on the problem(s) to solve often saves you a lot of wasted effort and frustration further down the line.

Too frequently we get excited about an idea and then implement it without really thinking through whether it solves a (significant) problem for our customers. Product management consultant and author Melissa Perri refers to this tendency as the build trap: a "move fast and break things" mindset that results when companies focus on what to build whilst forgetting to think about *why* they should build it. [12]

To avoid the build trap, I highly recommend starting with the why behind what you are intending to build. When working with a wide range of smart and passionate people, there is typically no lack of good ideas or solutions. Thinking about problems first will help you to make sure you are building the right thing for the right problem (and the right audience). So-called problem statements are a simple but effective way to focus on problems first and we will look at how to create problem statements in chapter 3.

6. The Difference between Project and Product Management

"What is the difference between project and product management?" is another question I am often asked. In response, I always focus on the life cycle aspect of product management. In traditional project management, the primary responsibility is to deliver a certain project within a set time frame and within an agreed budget and against a preagreed scope. [13] (See fig. 1.6.)

---

[12] "The Build Trap," Melissa Perri, August 5, 2014, https://melissaperri.com/blog/2014/08/05/the-build-trap.

[13] "What Is Project Management?" Association for Project Management, accessed February 3, 2018, https://www.apm.org.uk/resources/what-is-project-management/.

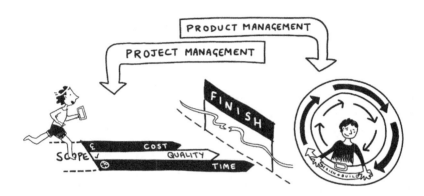

Figure 1.6. The continuous life cycle of most products is the biggest difference between product and project management.

In contrast, a product is never "done"; it is a constant evolution, always aiming to deliver more value to its users.[14] As a result, the job of a product manager is never done unless the decision is made to terminate a product. The traditional product life cycle consists of four stages, as depicted in figure 1.7: market development, market growth, market maturity, and market decline.[15]

- **Stage 1: Market development.** This is when a product is first brought to market. At this stage, demand for the product has not been proven yet. Sales are likely to be low.
- **Stage 2: Market growth.** Demand begins to accelerate, and there is a significant increase in market size.

---

[14] "Product Management Is Not Project Management," Spenser Skates, Mind the Product, January 8, 2018, https://www.mindtheproduct.com/2018/01/product-management-not-project-management/.
[15] Theodore Levitt, "Exploit the Product Life Cycle," *Harvard Business Review*, November 1965, accessed February 3, 2018, https://hbr.org/1965/11/exploit-the-product-life-cycle.

- **Stage 3: Market maturity.** Demand will reach a peak and then start to slow down. Sales growth will decrease, given that the product has reached market acceptance.
- **Stage 4: Market decline.** The product begins to lose consumer appeal, and sales start declining.

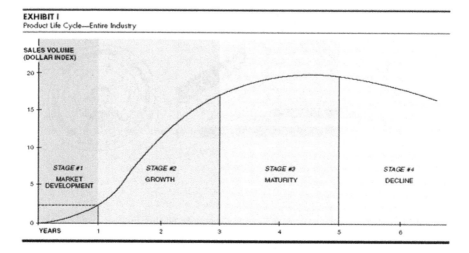

Figure 1.7. Theodore Levitt's product life cycle[16]

Experienced product managers will know that as a product evolves, their responsibilities and challenges will evolve accordingly. As a result, product management is an open-ended and broad discipline that is sometimes compared to acting as the CEO of a product.[17]

Although I don't entirely agree with that description (product managers often don't have even an inch of the authority a typical CEO has), product managers do bear a large responsibility for the direction and success of a product throughout its life cycle.

Key Takeaways

[16] Ibid.
[17] "Product Managers: Who Are These 'Mini-CEOs' and What Do They Do?" Ken Yeung, The Next Web, October 12, 2013, https://thenextweb.com/insider/2013/10/12/product-managers-mini-ceos/.

Whether they are digital or physical, products can be best described as tangible outputs that can be measured. As a product manager, you are ultimately responsible for the discovery and delivery of products that are usable and valuable to your (end) customers.

1. **Know the difference between digital and physical products.** A product can be physical or digital as long it delivers tangible value to the customer.
2. **Recognise the role of product management at the business intersection.** Product management is a critical business function, having to constantly balance customer needs with business interests and technological viability.
3. **Know the difference between product and project management.** In contrast to *project* management, a product is never done. Product managers are accountable for a product's performance throughout its life cycle.

How to Apply These Takeaways

- **Mention well-known digital and physical products to explain your role.** I have found that mentioning mainstream digital products, such as Facebook and Amazon.com, is very helpful in explaining what a digital product is. You can then contrast these examples with physical products, such as a Dyson Hoover or Samsung TV.
- **Position product management at the intersection of business to explain your role.** Especially if you have to explain to work colleagues unfamiliar with product management, you can look at the three different areas that product management spans: business, technology, and user experience. This helps you to then explain how you as a product manager bring these three areas together.
- **Outline the difference between product and project management to explain your role.** When explaining the differences between product and project management, I suggest highlighting the more on-off nature of most projects. This helps differentiate from product management, where development and learning are continuous until the product is discontinued.

2
What Makes a Good Product Manager?

Goal

To explore the common traits of what makes a good product manager.

Related Tools and Techniques to Consider

- Apply the **build-measure-learn feedback loop** to validate your assumptions and hypotheses with customers early and often.
- Be curious and ask the **5 Whys**.
- Consider the different stages of the **product life cycle** and manage your product accordingly.
- Create a **product vision**, which drives the **product strategy, road map**, and **backlog**.
- **Say no** in a clear but well-informed and constructive way.

Introduction

Having started exploring the fundamentals of product management, the next critical question is what are some of the common attributes you need as a product manager? What makes a good product manager? What are the common traits of a bad one?

This chapter will cover the core attributes that constitute good product management. We will delve into such aspects as value and curiosity. I will also contrast these attributes against common characteristics of so-called product janitors.

The following are the four key attributes of a good product manager:

- Customer focussed
- Value driven
- Curious
- Ability to learn and iterate

We will look at each of these traits in detail, understanding what they entail and how you can make them your own.

1. Focus on the Customer

Your website isn't the centre of your universe. Your Facebook page isn't the centre of your universe. Your mobile app isn't the centre of your universe. The customer is the centre of your universe.

—Ben Chestnut, cofounder and CEO of MailChimp

Being able to engage early and often with (prospective) customers is a non-negotiable skill for product managers. The main reason I feel so strongly about this is because my overarching view of product management begins and ends with the customer. Does this mean that as a product manager, you automatically build all the products or features that customers ask for or that you endlessly test with the customer before launching a product? Does soliciting customer feedback mean that your product is guaranteed to be a massive success? No is my emphatic answer to these questions.

It does mean, however, that you have a continuous feedback loop with your customers and that you learn from (non)customers throughout the product life cycle. Having this feedback loop in place helps you to mitigate the risk of creating a product that customers don't want or don't want to pay for. In the next chapter, we will look at some of the tools and techniques you can use to engage effectively with customers.

This is underscored by David Cancel, CEO at Drift, who states, "When you spend more time talking to 'internal stakeholders' than your customers, you've lost the ship."[18] Or as the late David Ogilvy, one of the founding fathers of modern advertising, put it, "The consumer is not a moron. She is your wife. Don't insult her intelligence."[19]

2. Value Driven: Customer Value and Business Value

In the previous chapter, I talked about creating a valuable product as the essence of product management. This raises the question of how to define value. How do you know whether your product is adding value? Who does the product deliver value for and why?

---

[18] "Creating a Customer-Driven Product Machine," David Cancel, October 29, 2014, http://davidcancel.com/customer-driven-product-machine.
[19] "David Ogilvy's Best Advice for Business," Patricia Sellers, *Fortune*, July 21, 2009, http://fortune.com/2009/07/21/david-ogilvys-best-advice-for-business/.

Customer Value

The customer ultimately perceives the value of your product. Whether you are managing a direct-to-consumer product or business-to-business product, the customer or end user ultimately defines the success of your product. (See fig. 2.1.)

Figure 2.1. Don't forget about what the customer actually wants.

In product management, there tend to be two schools of thought when it comes to thinking about the role and importance of the customer: build it and customers will come or get customer feedback early and often.

Build It and They Will Come

> *It's not the customer's job to know what they want.*
>
> —Steve Jobs

At one of my previous companies, a senior executive once told me, "Marc, if I were doing your role, I would probably do a lot less customer validation, as I know what customers want. I would just launch and see what happens."

My former colleague is not alone in this way of thinking. There is a school of thought amongst some product managers that you should trust your instinct to build the right product for your customers. People who follow this school of thought often refer to Henry Ford and his alleged quote that "If I'd asked my customers what they'd wanted, they'd have said a faster horse."[20] (See fig. 2.2.)

The late Steve Jobs is also a common reference when it comes to this way of thinking. He relied on his product instincts to create Apple's iPod and iPhone. Apparently, Jobs was not the biggest fan of focus groups: "It's really hard to design products by focus groups. A lot of times, people don't know what they want until you show it to them."[21]

[20] "What Henry Ford Can Teach Us about Product Management," Steve Keifer, Bantrr, April 12, 2010, https://bantrr.com/2010/04/12/what-henry-ford-can-teach-us-about-product-management/.
[21] "Why Steve Jobs Didn't Listen to His Customers," Gregory Ciotti, Help Scout, March 6, 2013, https://www.helpscout.net/blog/why-steve-jobs-never-listened-to-his-customers/.

Figure 2.2. Henry Ford believed that asking customers would have led only to having faster horses.

Focus groups are all about getting a group of customers in a room to get their views on a product and to have a discussion about it.[22] Jobs' line of reasoning suggests that customers don't know what they want or need until you present them with a solution.

Customer Validation: Early and Often

Products are sold because they solve a problem or fill a need. Understanding problems and needs involves understanding customers and what makes them tick.
—Steve Blank

In contrast, a customer-centric approach is all about validating a product and its underlying assumptions early and often with the customer. For example, do customers perceive the product to be valuable in solving their problems? Why (not)?

Steve Blank, author of *The Four Steps to the Epiphany*,[23] captures this approach best by highlighting the risk involved in the aforementioned build-it-and-they-will-come approach: "'Build and they will come,' is not a strategy, it's a prayer."[24]

Early in 2012, I attended a talk by Eric Ries, author of *The Lean Startup*,[25] in which he presented his thoughts in a jam-packed London auditorium. It became apparent that Ries had been inspired by Steve Blank's thinking when Ries talked about validated learning—a process where you take an initial idea and validate it with customers, measure its market influence, and iterate accordingly.[26] This approach is typified by a continuous build-measure-learn feedback loop, which signifies an iterative approach to product development. (See fig. 2.3.)[27]

---

[22] Powell, Richard A. and Single Helen M. "Focus groups," *International Journal of Quality in Health Care* 8, 5 (1996): 499–504.

[23] Steve Blank, *The Four Steps to the Epiphany: Successful Strategies for Products That Win*, 2nd ed. (Thermal, CA: K&S Ranch, 2013).

[24] Ibid., 7.

[25] Ries, *The Lean Startup*.

[26] "Why Build, Measure, Learn Isn't Just Throwing Things against the Wall to See if They Work—The Minimum Viable Product," Steve Blank, May 6, 2015, https://steveblank.com/2015/05/06/build-measure-learn-throw-things-against-the-wall-and-see-if-they-work/.

[27] "Methodology," The Lean Startup, accessed February 3, 2018, http://theleanstartup.com/principles.

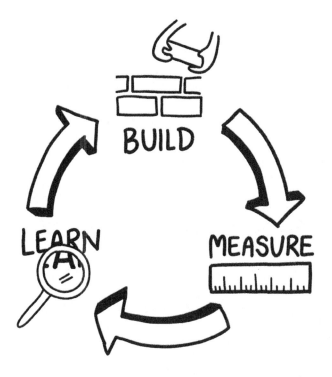

Figure 2.3. Developing successful products is a continuous and iterative process.

Instead of just shipping products or features as often as you can, the goal is to achieve and learn about specific user outcomes as frequently as possible. By applying the build-measure-learn feedback loop, you can learn quickly whether your product is actually changing customer behaviour.[28]

With the greatest of respect to Jobs and his views on customer feedback, I do believe it is critical to seek customer feedback early and often. Instead of simply

---

[28] "Jeff Gothelf and Lean UX," Marc Abraham, August 23, 2015, https://marcabraham.com/2015/08/23/jeff-gothelf-and-lean-ux/.

hoping that customers will buy your product, you get early indications from customers as to whether your idea or product meets their needs. In this day and age, the risk of just launching a product with the expectation that customers will buy it is one that most companies cannot afford to take.

Business Value

My simple adage is that customer value equals business value. In other words, a business is absolutely nowhere without customers. I therefore argue that as long as a product manager is successful in delivering customer value, business value is delivered as a direct result.

I realise full well that this equation might be a bit too simplistic. For example, product managers could provide customers with a great product that meets all their needs but that is underpriced and therefore not financially viable for the business. It is important for product managers to be aware of and achieve underlying business goals and metrics. In chapter 5, we will look at such aspects as managing risk and viability, giving you the tools required to fully deliver business value on a continuous basis.

3. Curiosity

If you do nothing else as a product manager, I urge you to ask why and to stay curious.[29] Why is curiosity such a vital aspect of product management?

I am sure there are plenty of product managers out there who refrain from asking questions but who still do an awesome job and are well respected within their organisations. (I'll talk about who I refer to as product janitors[30] later in this chapter.)

Why does curiosity contribute to being a good product manager?

- **Curiosity helps truly understand customer problems.** As a product manager, it is absolutely vital to fully understand the customer problem worth solving before exploring potential product solutions. "Love the

---

[29] "My Product Management Toolkit (19): Socratic Questioning," Marc Abraham, March 8, 2017, https://marcabraham.com/2017/03/08/my-product-management-toolkit-19-socratic-questioning/.

[30] "My Product Management Toolkit (16): How Not to become a 'Product Janitor'?," December 7, 2016, https://marcabraham.com/2016/12/07/my-product-management-toolkit-16-how-to-not-become-a-product-janitor/.

problem, not your solution," as Lean expert Ash Maurya aptly puts it.[31] This desire to understand customer problems helps to avoid building products nobody wants.

- **Curiosity helps find the best solution available to solve the problem identified.** Once you have established customer problems worth solving, the next challenge is to work out ways in which to solve a problem. In most cases, the solution will not necessarily be obvious, and you will need to explore, compare, and contrast a wide range of potential options—each presenting its own pros and cons.
- **Curiosity helps to unearth and validate assumptions and hypotheses.** By constantly asking why and understanding how your product is (not) solving customer problems, you will be able to identify and test key assumptions and hypotheses.
- **Curiosity helps avoid business inertia and products becoming obsolete.** In my experience, curiosity means that you are never resting on your laurels when it comes to creating great products or solving customer problems.

Curiosity is not something that can be taught. However, it is an important trait that can be developed. The easiest thing you can do to develop a sense of curiosity is to start by asking why.[32]

One of the first things I learned when I started in product management was the importance of asking why using the 5 Whys to truly understand a problem or situation: [33]

1. *Why?*—The battery is dead. (First why)
2. *Why?*—The alternator is not functioning. (Second why)
3. *Why?*—The alternator belt has broken. (Third why)
4. *Why?*—The alternator belt was well beyond its useful service life and not replaced. (Fourth why)
5. *Why?*—The vehicle was not maintained according to the recommended service schedule. (Fifth why, a root cause)

You will see how many ideas naturally follow that one simple word: *why*. Even though curiosity cannot be taught, it is something you can develop. In the next chapter, we will look at ways in which you can best channel this curiosity.

---

[31] "The BOOTSTART Manifesto," Ash Maurya, January 4, 2016, https://blog.leanstack.com/the-bootstart-manifesto-65b41da6216.

[32] "What I'm Learning about Hiring Good Product Managers," Marc Abraham, January 1, 2013, https://marcabraham.com/2013/01/01/what-im-learning-about-hiring-good-product-managers/.

[33] "5 Whys," *Wikipedia*, last edited January 26, 2018, https://en.wikipedia.org/wiki/5_Whys.

4. Iterative

Given the evolving nature of the product life cycle, product management is highly iterative in nature. It is very unlikely that at the end of the product life cycle a product is exactly the same as what it was at the start of it.

A case in point is the life cycle of Apple's iPod, which changed significantly from its inception in 2001 to its termination in 2013.[34] (See fig. 2.4.) Even with so-called big-bang disruptors,[35] where the traditional bell-shaped curve of the product life cycle is much shorter, there is likely to be an element of iterating on the initial product. Whether the product is a tractor or a mobile app, it is likely to evolve. Later we will see how customer data, feedback, and market trends drive product evolution and how you as a product manager can manage this evolution.

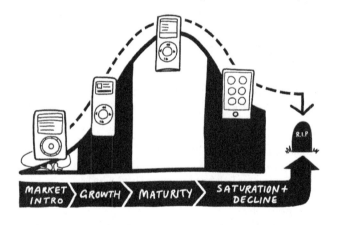

Figure 2.4. The evolution of the Apple iPod throughout its life cycle

5. What Good Product Management Is Not

[34] "Apple's iPod Life Cycle: The Four Phases," Ashley Truelove, Storify, accessed February 3, 2018, https://storify.com/Ash018/apple-s-ipod-life-cycle.
[35] Larry Downes and Paul Nunes, *Big Bang Disruption: Strategy in the Age of Devastating Innovation* (New York: Portfolio/Penguin, 2014).

In addition to understanding the key characteristics of good product management, it is just as important to explore when product management does not provide value to customers or the business.

It is important to pay attention to some of the traits and activities that sit outside of product management. We'll look at product janitors, the importance of saying no, and mini-CEOs.

Product Janitors

Because product management can be such a broadly defined role, there is a risk that product managers end up doing a bit of everything—mopping up the things that other team members do not want to do.

As a result, these product managers are unable to act effectively, by which I mean they fail to identify and manage products that are valuable, usable, and feasible. Steve Johnson, a well-known product management author and speaker, refers to these types of product managers as product janitors.[36] (See fig. 2.5.)

[36] Steve Johnson, *Look Beyond the Product: The Business of Agile Product Management* (North Charleston, SC: CreateSpace, 2014).

Figure 2.5. Avoid becoming a product janitor, simply mopping up stuff.

In my view, there are two key behaviours that make someone a product janitor: (1) doing all those things that other people do not want to do, or (2) always saying yes and trying to keep everyone happy.

Mopping up all the things the other team members don't want to do. As a product manager, there's a risk of getting distracted, which can take precious time away from such essentials as developing a product strategy or engaging with (potential) customers.

I have seen good product people end up as scrum masters, pastoral carers, testers, and dogsbodies for the product development teams of which they are a part. Instead of delegating responsibilities, some product managers seem to take up every possible task. Don't get me wrong; product management is inherently a very broad role, with product managers rightly expected to pull their sleeves up and solve problems.

However, the breadth of some product management roles prevents enthusiastic and well-meaning individuals from doing justice to the multifaceted character of product management. Often it forces people to end up optimising only one aspect of product management, most commonly resulting in them spending their time concentrating on, for example, technology (at the detriment of user experience or commercials).

Product management is, by its very nature, about collaborating with and managing a wide range of stakeholders and their interests. Although I have nothing against colleagues helping one another out and collaborating, I would be careful about picking tasks or responsibilities purely because no one else is doing them.

Always saying yes. Granted, it can be hard to say no to people. However, I'm afraid that as a product person, you'll simply have to! If you don't say no, or at least ask why, there's a risk you'll end up shepherding someone else's user stories or requirements and nothing more. When I am looking to hire good product people, I want to meet people who feel comfortable saying no. People who have a clear product vision and a strategy to achieve the vision. People who aren't afraid to make tough decisions, which Roman Pichler refers to as the difference between a big product owner and a small product owner.[37] (See fig. 2.6.)

Figure 2.6. Roman Pichler's big product owner versus small product owner comparison[38]

---

[37] "Size Matters: Big vs. Small Product Owner," Roman Pichler, June 23, 2015,
http://www.romanpichler.com/blog/big-product-owner-small-product-owner/.
[38] Ibid.

In conclusion, I see two main ways through which you can avoid becoming a product janitor.

Carve out time to create a product vision, strategy, and road map. Having a clear product vision, strategy, and road map can help safeguard yourself against becoming the steward of someone else's backlog. The chances of you just cleaning up someone else's mess become slimmer if you have a clear vision, strategy, and road map that drive your everyday activities.

If you are working at a small start-up, you're bound to wear multiple hats. However, you can still be selective about the number and type of hats you decide to wear and how you balance them. Having a clear understanding about what you are trying to achieve combined with a clear underlying rationale will help.

How to best say no. Saying no doesn't have to be painful. There are several reasons to say no to an idea or request, even if it sounds compelling. Learning how to best say no is one of the key things I've learned over the last few years. In chapter 5, we will look more in depth at ways in which you can best say no as a product manager.

6. Busting Some Common Myths about Product Managers

I hope that by now you have a better understanding of both product management fundamentals and what makes a good product manager. However, it will help to look at some of the common myths and misconceptions that seem to surround product management.

Myth 1: Product managers should have all the answers or great ideas. I attribute the expectation that product managers are all-knowing to the late, great Steve Jobs. Of course, Jobs turned out to be an amazing product person, but (1) he was surrounded by extremely talented product developers and designers,[39] and (2) Apple *did* and still does conduct market and customer research.[40] This is just one example of how even the most proven of product people relied both on an amazing team and on customer insights. Good product managers are, first and foremost,

---

[39] "Walter Isaacson: Steve Jobs' Favourite Product Was the Team He Built at Apple," Big Think Editors, Big Think, accessed February 3, 2018, http://bigthink.com/think-tank/steve-jobs-as-prickly-team-builder-with-walter-isaacson.
[40] "How Apple Conducts Market Research and Keeps iOS Source Code Locked Down," Yoni Heisler, Network World, August 3, 2012, http://www.networkworld.com/article/2222892/wireless/how-apple-conducts-market-research-and-keeps-ios-source-code-locked-down.html.

very, very good at listening.[41] As Peter Drucker noted, "The most important thing in communication is hearing what isn't said."

Myth 2: Product managers are rock stars. Much like my previous point about product managers being, product managers aren't just brilliant soloists. By their very nature, they are not rock stars and cannot act alone. To stick with the music analogy, product managers are always part of a band and need to work closely with all the band members, fans, record label execs, roadies, sound crew, and so forth all-knowing to create the best outcomes for the customer and the business. (See fig. 2.7.)

Figure 2.7. Product managers aren't rock stars; they wouldn't be able to perform without their band, crew, and fans.

Myth 3: Product managers are all about delivery and execution. "Don't mistake activity for achievement" is a brilliant quote from the late John Wooden, probably

41 "Book Review: 'The Art of Active Listening,'" Marc Abraham, April 13, 2017, https://marcabraham.com/2017/04/13/book-review-the-art-of-active-listening/; "The Importance of Listening to Your Customers by David Cancel," Martin Eriksson, Mind the Product, December 2, 2016, http://www.mindtheproduct.com/2016/12/importance-listening-customers-david-cancel/.

the most successful college basketball coach in the United States.[42] Wooden's point was that it is much more important to ask yourself whether you have come closer to achieving your goals than to solely look at your activities or output.

Good product managers don't just concentrate on getting stuff done. Instead, their focus is on getting the right things done for the right audience and for the right reasons. This, in my view, comprises both delivery and learning. I would go one step further by stating that continuous discovery is almost as important as continuous delivery.[43]

Myth 4: Product managers are mini-CEOs. This has been a topic of much debate in the product management community.[44] For what it's worth, I disagree with those people who believe the role of product management is similar to that of a CEO. When I started out as a product manager, I was very keen to believe that I was the CEO of my product.

A good number of years later, I now see that this was an illusion. I am not the CEO of my product and will probably never be. As product managers, we are often not in charge of our own destinies and don't have the same level of authority (or accountability) that most CEOs have.

Nevertheless, I do view product managers as being fully accountable for the success of their products. For example, when a product does not see the light of day or fails to deliver value for its customers, then the buck stops with the responsible product manager.

Key Takeaways

Developing a sense of curiosity and understanding of customer value are great places to start if you are looking to become a good product manager. I strongly

---

[42] "If You Want to Be Successful, Don't Confuse Being Busy with Getting the Right Things Done," Paul B. Brow, *Forbes*, December 14, 2013, https://www.forbes.com/sites/actiontrumpseverything/2013/12/14/if-you-want-to-be-successful-dont-confuse-being-busy-with-getting-the-right-things-done/.

[43] "My Product Management Toolkit (13): Continuous Discovery," Marc Abraham, August 20, 2016, https://marcabraham.com/2016/08/20/my-product-management-toolkit-13-continuous-discovery/.

[44] "Product Managers—You Are Not the CEO of Anything," Martin Eriksson, Mind the Product, March 15, 2017, http://www.mindtheproduct.com/2017/03/product-managers-not-ceo-anything/; "Stop Saying Product Management Is Like Being the CEO of Your Own Product," Ale Carlos, Medium, September 9, 2015, https://medium.com/@alecarlos/stop-saying-product-management-is-like-being-the-ceo-of-your-own-product-c7c78b0ba76f; "Good Product Manager/Bad Product Manager," Ben Horowitz, June 15, 2012, https://a16z.com/2012/06/15/good-product-managerbad-product-manager/.

believe that good product management boils down to asking why and wanting to understand customer problems fully.

1. **It's all about customer value.** Creating tangible customer value is paramount as a product manager.
2. **Stay curious.** Curiosity underpins everything you do as product manager. Start by asking why.
3. **Don't become a product janitor.** A product janitor is someone who just picks up the slack left by others.

How to Apply These Takeaways

- **Prove customer value when confronted with an attitude of 'we know what customers want.'** Even in situations when there is no opportunity to learn from customers *before* launching a product or feature, the only way to rebuff people who believe that customers don't know what they want is to provide them with data—qualitative and quantitative—about customer problems (not) solved through your product.
- **Ask why when you want to understand.** The simplest way to start understanding a problem or proposed solution is by asking why, ideally five times (the 5 Whys). You will see how the discipline of constant questioning will help you to fully understand a problem or what someone else is proposing. For example, if someone claims, "That is never going to work," asking why will give you his or her rationale for that statement, which you can then address.
- **Apply the build-measure-learn feedback loop when launching a new product.** Be iterative and avoid spending a large amount of time designing and building the perfect solution. Take into account that most products are evolving constantly, along with customer needs and market developments. If you are, for example, presented with a great opportunity to disrupt an existing industry, don't spend too much time building a product in total isolation. Instead, make full use of the build-measure-learn feedback loop to create a product that can evolve throughout its own life cycle.

3
Engaging with and Learning from Customers

Goal

To learn how we can engage with and learn from our customers continuously without having to break the bank or spend heaps of time doing research.

Related Tools and Techniques to Consider

- Apply **customer segmentation** to better understand who your customers are.
- Implement **user personas** to help understand certain customer demographics and behaviours, provided you *validate* your personas.
- Use **empathy maps** to capture what customers think and feel.
- Use **problem statements** to identify and communicate customer problems.
- Focus on customer outcomes by using the **jobs-to-be-done framework**.
- Conduct **customer interviews** and carry out direct **observations**, two cost-effective ways to quickly learn more about your customers and their needs.

Introduction

Don't make a better [X], make a better [user of X].

—Kathy Sierra

My hope is that, by now, I have convinced you of the importance of engaging with your (target) customers. Ultimately, successful products are those products that are bought and used. By whom? By people, your customers. You might feel that I am pointing out the obvious here, but you will be surprised how often customers are overlooked when it comes to developing products.[45]

Engaging with and learning from customers is an ongoing activity throughout the entire product life cycle, and you are likely to want to learn different things at different stages. I call this "continuous discovery" to highlight that ongoing learning drives product development.

However, I have come across plenty of product managers who don't speak to their customers. When I probe to further understand why this is the case, people explain

---

[45] "My Product Management Toolkit (13): Continuous Discovery," Marc Abraham, August 20, 2016, https://marcabraham.com/2016/08/20/my-product-management-toolkit-13-continuous-discovery/.

that "We know what customers want"[46] or that "Customer research is hard and expensive."

In this chapter, we'll see how important customers are to product managers, and I'll provide some concrete tools and techniques you can use to get started on customer research.

1. Why Everything Begins and Ends with Customers

"Will my customer use this?"

"Will my customer pay for this?"

These two very simple but incredibly powerful sentences should underpin everything you do or think about as a product manager.

In the previous chapter, I stressed the value of asking why. Once again, the *why* question is critical if you wish to understand fully why your customers are (not) buying or using your product:

"Will my customer use this?" **Why (not)?**

"Will my customer pay for this?" **Why (not)?**

Whether you like it or not, customers will determine the success of your product. This does not mean that you should automatically do whatever the customer tells you to do. Product management is not like Christmas. It is not about customers giving you their wish lists, and you are not Father Christmas. (See fig. 3.1.)

I came across a company once that had asked its customers during an in-house event which products they would like to see created. The customers could dot vote on big sheets of paper that each had a product on it. The contest was clearly won by the API. However, as soon as the company had built and released the API, it turned out it was not what customers had wanted. The company learned that customers thought that the API stood for some sort of system that would make it easier for them to manage their stock and orders. Several customers admitted that they hadn't fully understood what API meant but had voted for it because their

---

[46] This explanation is effectively the same as the build-it-and-they-will-come rationale mentioned in the previous chapter.

peers had encouraged them to do so. The moral of this story is to invest in truly understanding your customers and their needs.

Figure 3.1. Product management is not about fulfilling customer wish lists.

If product management is not about automatically fulfilling customer wishes, how do we listen to our customers and make sure we meet their needs? There are two core questions that we as product managers need to be able to answer. Firstly, who are my customers? Secondly, what are their needs? Getting a handle on your customers and their needs is instrumental in creating great products that solve customer problems. I refer to this as a process of continuous discovery, which highlights the ongoing nature of customer learning.

2. Who Are My Customers?

When you are fully immersed in the day-to-day hustle and bustle of product management, it can be easy to forget about the customer or to simply assume that you know who your customers are and what they want.

This is a dangerous trap to fall into. Customers are not static personas; their needs, characteristics, and contexts are likely to evolve over time. Before you can effectively solve customer problems, you need to know who your target audience is.[47]

---

[47] "My Product Management Toolkit (8): Learning Who My Users Are," Marc Abraham, April 8, 2016, https://marcabraham.com/2016/04/08/my-product-management-toolkit-8-learning-who-my-users-are/.

There are several ways in which you can learn about and capture who your customers are. Over time I have found that customer segmentation, persona development, empathy mapping, and identifying jobs to be done are four effective ways to understand customer profiles.

Customer Segmentation

Customer segmentation is the process of dividing potential markets or customers into specific groups. This process typically feeds into companies' marketing efforts and product strategies. There are several different ways in which you can segment your customer base:

- **A priori:** This commonly used form of customer segmentation is based on theory rather than on market or customer research.[48] Apart from theory, people also use assumptions or hunches to break down markets into specific groups.[49] For example, deducing that adults over seventy years old do not drive as much as twenty-year-olds based on the reasoning that driving becomes harder after a certain age due to common mobility or eyesight issues seems like a safe assumption to make. However, this is still an assumption and not underpinned by any form of research.
- **Usage or behavioural segmentation:** With usage or behavioural segmentation, customer segments are based on their different needs and levels of consumption of a particular product or service.[50] For example, you could compare the amount of spaghetti consumed by an adult to the amount eaten by a toddler.
- **Demographic segmentation:** This is a common way of doing customer segmentation and typically divides a group of people based on specific variables, such as profession, age, gender, income, nationality, race, religion, and income size. There are several tools in the market that can help inform some of these demographic insights.[51]
- **Psychographic segmentation:** This form of segmentation uses people's lifestyles and their activities and opinions to define a customer segment. Psychographic segmentation is similar to the previously mentioned usage or

---

[48] "A Priori," Insights Association, accessed February 3, 2018, http://www.insightsassociation.org/issues-policies/glossary/priori.
[49] J. A. Lunn, "Consumer Decision-Process Models," in *Models of Buyer Behavior*, ed. Jagdish N. Sheth (New York: Harper & Row, 1974), 34–69.
[50] "Usage Based Segmentation and Its Application in Marketing," Hitesh Bhasin, Marketing 91, December 25, 2017, http://www.marketing91.com/usage-based-segmentation/.
[51] See, for example, "Mosaic in Detail," Experian, accessed February 3, 2018, http://www.experian.co.uk/marketing-services/products/mosaic/mosaic-in-detail.html; "Understanding Consumers and Communities," Acorn, accessed February 3, 2018, https://acorn.caci.co.uk/what-is-acorn.

behavioural segmentation, but it also considers the psychological aspects of consumer buying behaviour.

- **Geographic segmentation:** This type of market segmentation divides people on the basis of geography. Your potential customers will have different needs based on where they are located.

Persona Development

> *You don't design personas; you discover them.*
>
> —Alan Cooper

Personas can provide a good overview of who your users are. Personas were introduced in 1998 by Alan Cooper[52] and are effective design tools—making it easier to ensure you're designing and creating the right product for the right person.

Personas are effectively stories involving imagined characters. (See the example in fig. 3.2.) In these fictitious stories, you can include such details as the age, occupation, or pain points of the customer in question. Having clear personas can effectively help create a shared language across the organisation as can conducting research with the right customer types.

However, a word of warning about personas is in order for three reasons. Firstly, I have seen numerous cases where personas were created as a one-off exercise, never to be really looked at or revisited afterward. Personas are effective only if you use them actively and update them as you learn more about your real-life customers.

Secondly, I often find that personas don't do enough justice to the specific problems we need to solve for our customers or their key activities. This is mostly because personas are made up. Thus the risk with personas is that they can become fairly flat and incompatible with reality. As a result, you might end up building a product for a customer who does not exist. Empathy mapping and the jobs-to-be-done framework are two techniques that cover these limitations of user personas.

Thirdly, it is a misconception that user personas are to be developed or used within the exclusive domain of a single organisational department, such as in design or product management. For personas to be powerful, they need to be used across the

---

[52] "The Origin of Personas," Alan Cooper, May 15, 2008, https://www.cooper.com/journal/2008/05/the_origin_of_personas.

organisation. For example, marketing messages should be crafted based on the same persona for which the product has been built. Similarly, the collateral that sales teams use should be based on the same person.

Figure 3.2. User persona example: fictitious demographics, needs, and behaviours that all must be validated

Empathy Mapping

Want your users to fall in love with your designs? Fall in love with your users.
—Dana Chisnell

Empathy does not automatically mean that you should fall in love with your customers, as Dana Chisnell suggested in the previous quote. However, even if you don't go as far as loving your customers, empathy does mean that you should go as far as you can to put yourself in their shoes.

I have found empathy mapping to be a great way of capturing insights into another person's thoughts, feelings, perceptions, pain, gains, and behaviours.[53] Similar to

[53] "Updated Empathy Map Canvas," Dave Gray, Medium, July 15, 2017, https://medium.com/the-xplane-collection/updated-empathy-map-canvas-46df22df3c8a.

user personas, empathy maps tend to be most effective when they have been created collectively and validated continuously with actual customers.

These are the common components of an empathy map:

- **Thinking and feeling:** What is the customer thinking and feeling and why? You must understand customer needs and how customers feel about those needs. It is about figuring out what really matters to the customer and why. Let's use a fictitious app called EasySave. Target customers might think, "I want to see my spending information on a daily basis so that I don't spend too much money and run out of cash." A statement like this then enables you to probe and learn *why* there is a risk of people running out of cash if they don't view their spending information on a daily basis and how they feel about that.
- **Seeing:** What is the customer seeing, either in the market, around him or her, or from friends or family? A potential EasySave customer could observe, "I see a lot of personal finance management apps, but none of them are easy to use."
- **Hearing:** Similar to seeing, what is the customer hearing from his or her friends, family, colleagues, or influencers? For example, "My friends keep telling me that the EasySave app is very simple to use."
- **Saying:** What are customers saying in public and why? What is their attitude toward a product or problem? For example, customers could leave a negative online review about the EasySave app in which they complain that they were none the wiser about their financial situations after using the app.

Empathy maps effectively capture and visualise your insights or assumptions about your (target) audience. Much like personas (and especially if your empathy map is based on assumptions), it is important to treat the empathy map as a living document and not as a one-off exercise. Customer needs and behaviours are likely to evolve, and it is important to keep reflecting these evolutions in your empathy map.

3. What Are My Customers' Problems?

If I had an hour to solve a problem I'd spend 55 minutes thinking about the problem and 5 minutes thinking about solutions.

—Albert Einstein

Having developed empathy for your (target) customers should make it easier to understand their problems and the results of these problems on their daily lives.

A problem statement is a simple but effective way to concentrate on the key problem(s) to solve, constantly asking the why of a specific customer problem or need. One thing I realised when using problem statements for the first time is an almost innate tendency to include a potential solution in the statement. Starting out as a product manager, I quickly learned that it is important to refrain from including solutions in your problem statements and to restrict yourself to the user problem instead.

Here is a standard problem statement formula:

> Stakeholder (describe person using empathetic language) NEEDS A WAY TO Need (needs are verbs) BECAUSE Insight (describe what you've learned about the stakeholder and his or her need).

The following are some simple examples:

> Richard, who loves to eat biscuits, wants to find a way to eat five biscuits a day without gaining weight, as he's currently struggling to keep his weight under control.

> Sandra from the Frying Pan Company, who likes using our data platform, wants to be able to see the sales figures of her business for the previous three years so that she can do accurate stock planning for the coming year.

As you can see from these simple examples, the idea is that you put yourself in the shoes of your (target) users and ask yourself, "So what? What is the effect that we're looking to have on a user's life? Why?"

A problem statement is not meant to be a solution in disguise. The idea is not to come up with a solution in your statement. In contrast, problem statements need to reflect your understanding of the problem that you're looking to solve and serve as a communication tool in ensuring that other people are on the same page with regard to understanding a problem. The following outlines the main functions of a problem statement:[54]

---

[54] "Stage 2 in the Design Thinking Process: Define the Problem and Interpret the Results," Rikke Dam and Teo Siang, Interaction Design Foundation, accessed February 3, 2018, https://www.interaction-design.org/literature/article/stage-2-in-the-design-thinking-process-define-the-problem-and-interpret-the-results.

A good problem statement:

- provides focus and frames the problem, being narrow enough to make the problem manageable;
- inspires and empowers your team, offering the creative freedom to work out the best way to solve the problem and implement a solution; and
- captures the hearts and minds of people you meet, framing the problem according to specific users and their needs. The problem statement is all about the people who you are looking to help.

Using problem statements to understand and validate the problems you are looking to solve is an important tool in every product manager's toolkit. Critical product decisions, such as evaluating product ideas, are helped enormously by a shared understanding of the specific problems to resolve.

4. What Do My Customers Need?

Jobs-to-Be-Done Framework

> *People don't buy quarter inch drills; they buy quarter inch holes.*
>
> —Theodor Levitt

The jobs-to-be-done framework helps you to better understand the problems you are trying to solve for your customers. This framework was originally put forward by Clayton Christensen and was advanced by the likes of Alan Klement and Bob Moesta.[55] In the words of Stephen Wunker, Jessica Wattman, and David Farber, "Once you understand what jobs people are striving to do, it becomes easier to predict what products or services they will take up and which will fall flat."[56]

With the aforementioned user personas and empathy maps, you should have a much better understanding of *who* your customers are; by looking at customer jobs, you

---

[55] "The 'Jobs to Be Done' Theory of Innovation," Clayton Christensen, *Harvard Business Review*, December 8, 2016, https://hbr.org/ideacast/2016/12/the-jobs-to-be-done-theory-of-innovation.html; "Replacing the User Story with the Job Story," Alan Klement, Medium, November 12, 2013, https://jtbd.info/replacing-the-user-story-with-the-job-story-af7cdee10c27; "Uncovering the Jobs to Be Done," Bob Moesta and Chris Spiek, Business of Software, June 12, 2014, http://businessofsoftware.org/2014/06/bos-2013-bob-moesta-and-chris-spiek-uncovering-the-jobs-to-be-done/.

[56] Stephen Wunker, Jessica Wattman, and David Farber, *Jobs to Be Done: A Roadmap for Customer-Centered Innovation* (New York: Amacom, 2016), 17.

will get a better understanding of customer *problems* and their influence on the customer:

- What job is the customer looking to get done and why?
- How is the customer getting this job done? What is the result?
- What jobs are customers not doing and why? What is the result?

For example:

- What job is the customer looking to get done and why? **Getting the car cleaned.**
- How is the customer getting this job done? What is the result? **Going to the car wash or doing it oneself. Both methods are time-consuming, and going to the car wash is expensive.**
- What jobs are customers not doing and why? What is the result? **Taking the family out for a fun activity. Quality time with the family is affected.**

Strategic thinkers Tony Ulwick and Lance Bettencourt identified three validating questions to help map the steps customers take to accomplish a specific outcome:[57]

- **Defining the execution step:** What are the most central tasks that must be accomplished in getting the job done?
- **Defining the pre-execution steps:** What must happen before the core execution step to ensure the job is successfully carried out?
- **Defining the postexecution steps:** What must happen after the core execution step to ensure the job is successfully carried out?

One of the things I really like about the jobs-to-be-done framework is the focus on user outcomes, the so-what element of the typical job statement:[58]

When _____ I want to _____ So I can _____
(situation)   (motivation)   (expected outcome)

The jobs-to-be-done framework outlines the eight steps that most jobs have in common:

---

[57] Lance Bettencourt and Anthony W. Ulwick, "The Customer-Centered Innovation Map," *Harvard Business Review*, May 2008, accessed February 3, 2018, https://hbr.org/2008/05/the-customer-centered-innovation-map.
[58] "Designing Features Using Job Stories," Alan Klement, Intercom, accessed February 3, 2018, https://blog.intercom.io/using-job-stories-design-features-ui-ux/.

- **Step 1: Define.** Customers determine their goals and plan their resources.
- **Step 2: Locate.** Customers gather items and information needed to do the job.
- **Step 3: Prepare.** Set up the environment for customers to do their jobs.
- **Step 4: Confirm.** Verify that customers are ready to perform the job.
- **Step 5: Execute.** Customers carry out the job without any problems or delays.
- **Step 6: Monitor.** Assess whether the job is being successfully executed.
- **Step 7: Modify.** Make alterations to improve execution.
- **Step 8: Conclude.** Finish the job or prepare to repeat it.

The following list contains several fictitious examples of the jobs-to-be-done framework: [59]

- **Example of define (step 1):** I need to find a quick way to understand my monthly mobile phone bill and how to spend less on mobile phone bills. Perhaps looking at the top line items on my bill can help in figuring this out. **How can a company help customers at the define stage?** Create a real-time version online of customers' mobile phone bills where they can quickly and easily scan their mobile phone bill breakdown.

- **Example of locate (step 2):** I need a quick view of how much I've spent this month on text messages and international calls.
  How can a company help customers at the locate stage? Colour-code those cost components of the mobile phone bill where the customer is of exceeding what's covered in his or her contractual package with the mobile provider.

- **Example of prepare (step 3):** When I look at my billing information, I need to know the specific phone numbers I've called or texted.
  How can a company help customers at the prepare stage? By making it as easy as possible for customers to find information about numbers called or texted. For example, if a customer has made multiple calls to the same number over a certain time period.

- **Example of confirm (step 4):** I would like to get a reminder to look at my mobile phone usage before an automatic payment is made on my monthly

[59] "My Product Management Toolkit (10): Jobs-to-Be-Done," Marc Abraham, June 2, 2016, https://marcabraham.com/2016/06/02/my-product-management-toolkit-10-jobs-to-be-done/.

phone bill so that I have time to review and raise any issues with my mobile carrier.

How can a company help customers at the confirm stage? Send customers a push notification seven days before the monthly invoice is sent out to remind customers to check usage and to make any package changes, including a link to the real-time data.

- **Example of execute (step 5):** The billing information I am looking at needs to be as current as possible. It's no good to me if the data are more than a day out.

  How can a company help customers at the execute stage? Ensure that there are no lags in the data provided, thus maintaining optimal performance.

- **Example of monitor (step 6):** I expect my mobile carrier to share a report of my last logins into personal billing information across locations and devices so that I can discover any suspicious login activity as early as possible.

  How can a company help customers at the monitor stage? Putting analytics in place—both for desktop and mobile—to monitor data usage on an ongoing basis.

- **Example of modify (step 7):** I'd like personalised billing information based on my previous viewing behaviours or enquiries.

  How can a company help customers at the modify stage? By personalising the data presented to customers, the mobile phone provider will save customers from having to wade through lots of data or having to customise data themselves.

- **Example of conclude (step 8):** I've seen my real-time billing information and will now log out.

  How can a company help customers at the conclude stage? Provide customers with appropriate calls to action once they've viewed their billing information—for example, contacting customer service.

One of the biggest benefits of the jobs-to-be-done framework is that it helps to understand value for the customer. It is often too easy to simply assume customer value. In my experience, the jobs-to-be-done framework puts a spotlight on the outcomes customers are trying to achieve and the relative importance of these outcomes.

I see these as the main benefits of the jobs-to-be-done approach, several elements of which will be discussed in the next section:

- It helps you to understand value for the customer.
- It identifies the progress users are (or aren't) making toward their desired job outcomes.
- It focusses people on outcomes and needs instead of on solutions.
- It takes user context into account. (For example, *where* does the customer get the job done?)
- It helps you to concentrate user research on what users actually do instead of on what they *say* they do.
- It enables you to distinguish between the main job to be done and related ones and to prioritise accordingly.

5. Who Are Your Customers, and What Are Their Needs?

There are several ways in which you can find out who your customers are or validate your assumptions about them. You could, for example, send out a survey with a set number of questions. If you have a larger budget, you could take this one step further and buy customer or market data from specialised providers.

At a high level, there are three ways in which you can group the different customer research methods available. These three distinctions are as follows:

1. **Behavioural versus attitudinal:** This distinction is about learning what people say (attitudinal) as opposed to what people do.[60] For example, a user interview is a good way to learn more about a customer's opinion (attitudinal), whereas observing a customer whilst he or she is using your product provides insight into a user's actions (behavioural).
2. **Quantitative versus qualitative:** When doing quantitative customer research, you typically use a survey or analytics software to learn more indirectly about customer behaviour. Analytics tools, such as Google Analytics or Mixpanel, enable you to study data on how customers are behaving, looking for patterns in the data.[61] In contrast, you learn about customers by either speaking to them or observing them *directly*.

---

[60] "When to Use Which User-Experience Research Methods," Christian Rohrer, Nielsen Norman Group, October 12, 2014, https://www.nngroup.com/articles/which-ux-research-methods/.
[61] "Some Considerations Regarding Data-Driven Design," Marc Abraham, September 9, 2013, https://marcabraham.com/2013/09/09/some-considerations-regarding-data-driven-design/.

3. **Generative versus evaluative:** Generative research focusses on learning about customer pain points and identifying opportunities for innovation. For example, observing users can be a good way to learn more about customers firsthand. Evaluative research comes into play if you wish to test your existing solution with customers.[62]

One could easily dedicate an entire book to customer research, and there are indeed some great books out there on this topic.[63] If you are interested in more extensive customer research, the following are some common research approaches:

- **Interview:** When interviewing your (target) users, listening is absolutely key.[64] I've seen product people make the mistake of using conversations with customers to confirm their assumptions, hearing only what they want to hear. When conducted well, interviews can be a rich source of product ideas and allow you to learn about user needs.
- **Observation:** One of the reasons why I always like to observe people in their own habitats is that it provides an opportunity to truly understand their current behaviour without your product or service.[65] Does the user really have the problem that your product is looking to address? Is it as big a problem for the user as you think it is? If so, why? Reframer is a good example of a tool you can use to note down your observations.
- **Diary study:** With a diary study, participants document their activities, thoughts, decisions, and opinions over a period of time. The main benefit of this technique is that it gives you good insight into what your users actually do and think. As UX expert Tomer Sharon mentions in his book *Validating Product Ideas*, "It reveals behaviour that would be hard to remember in interviews or surveys."[66]
- **Survey:** Online survey tools, such as SurveyMonkey and Typeform, provide a quick and easy way to learn from a large number of users within a short space of time. The main downside of surveys, however, is that you're

---

[62] "Generative vs. Evaluative Research: What's the Difference and Why Do We Need Each?," Janelle Estes, UserTesting, December 17, 2015, https://www.usertesting.com/blog/2015/12/17/generative-vs-evaluative-research/.
[63] See, for example, Erika Hall, *Just Enough Research* (New York: A Book Apart, 2013); Steve Krug, *Rocket Surgery Made Easy: The Do-It-Yourself Guide to Finding and Fixing Usability Problems* (Berkeley, CA: New Riders, 2010); Cennydd Bowles and James Box, *Undercover User Experience Design* (Berkeley, CA: New Riders, 2011); James Lang and Emma Howell, *Researching UX: User Research* (Victoria, Australia: SitePoint, 2017).
[64] "How to Do Effective User Interviews?" Marc Abraham, April 20, 2014, https://marcabraham.com/2014/04/20/how-to-do-effective-user-interviews/.
[65] "Designing for Behavior Change Book Review," Marc Abraham, Nir and Far, accessed February 3, 2018, https://www.nirandfar.com/2014/08/designing-for-behavior-change-book-review.html.
[66] Tomer Sharon, *Validating Product Ideas through Lean User Research* (Brooklyn, NY: Rosenfeld Media, 2016).

limited in exploring the real depth of why. Interviews and observations can be more effective in this respect.

- **Experience sampling:** Experience sampling helps you to learn about how customers react or feel at the exact moment when a certain event happens.[67] In an experience sampling study, research participants are interrupted several times a day or week to note their experiences in real time. For example, you could observe how customers react every time they come home from work. What do they do? What do they say? How do they feel? Getting the timing right and repeating the observation is critical if you want to reduce the risk of people speculating about expected behaviour.[68]

You might have noticed that I haven't included focus groups in this list. This is purely because I am not a big fan of focus groups. In focus group sessions, a group of users has an open discussion about a new product or service and gives their feedback. This is a very artificial construct that allows people to discuss a product in circumstances that are far removed from how they would normally use the product.[69] In addition, groupthink, whereby participants censor or change their opinions to conform to the group, can stop people from giving their honest opinions about a product.[70]

6. When and How to Conduct Customer Interviews

"It's too time-consuming to speak to customers" or "It's too expensive" are two of the most commonly voiced objections I hear when I ask people about speaking to their (target) customers. Customer interviews defy these objections.

Firstly, it is often not particularly difficult to find a couple of customers—or potential customers, if your product is at a very early stage—to talk to. I often find that my customer learnings start duplicating after I have spoken with five

[67] Stephen Intille, Charles Kukla, and Xiaoyi Ma, "Eliciting User Preferences Using Image-Based Experience Sampling and Reflection," in *Proceedings of the CHI '02 Extended Abstracts on Human Factors in Computing Systems* (New York: ACM Press, 2002), 738–39.

[68] "Context-Aware Experience Sampling," Massachusetts Institute of Technology, accessed February 3, 2018, http://web.mit.edu/caesproject/; "Experience Sampling Method," Wikipedia, last edited November 7, 2017, https://en.wikipedia.org/wiki/Experience_sampling_method.

[69] See also "Focus Groups Are Worthless," Erika Hall, Medium, September 22, 2014, https://medium.com/research-things/focus-groups-are-worthless-7d30891e58f1.

[70] Martha Ann Carey and Mickey W. Smith, "Capturing the Group Effect in Focus Groups: A Special Concern in Analysis," *Qualitative Health Research* 4, no. 1 (1994): 123–27.

customers.[71] A short conversation with five different customers is often easy to arrange, whether you meet in person or use the phone or a free conferencing tool.[72]

Secondly, speaking to customers does not have to be expensive. Picking up the phone to speak to customers or inviting a few over is pretty easy to do. Even if you speak to just five (target) customers, you will be able to get valuable customer feedback. If you have dedicated customers, you might not have to pay them for their time and input, and covering travel expenses or offering a gift voucher will likely be sufficient. I would always argue that the cost and risk of not speaking to customers is likely to outweigh the limited cost of interacting with customers on a regular basis.

I know many product managers who worry about speaking to customers, either because they are concerned about committing to features or because they are not entirely sure what to ask. Over the years I have learned some of the dos and don'ts when conducting user interviews:[73]

1. **Ask yourself what you want to get out of the user interview.** A key part of the effectiveness of user interviews is in the preparation. There are two critical aspects to the interview prep. First is defining the more *strategic* outcomes you would like to get out of the user interviews. What is it that you want to learn from the user? Which user or business assumptions do you wish to validate?[74] You can use these kinds of questions to formulate the goals of your user interviews. In his book *Inspired: How to Create Products Customers Love*, product management expert Marty Cagan outlines how one can utilise user interviews (or other product discovery techniques) to help answer some important product questions. Secondly, preparing all the different *practicalities* involved in user interviews is just as crucial an aspect of user interviews as the way in which you run these sessions. Following this list, I've put together some practical ideas you might want to consider.

2. **Avoid leading questions.** I've learned to refrain from asking users such questions as "Do you prefer option A, with its rich set of features, or the more limited option B?" or "Would you use this product if it were free?" Questions like these almost constitute a cardinal sin when it comes to

[71] See also "Why You Only Need to Test with 5 Users," Jakob Nielsen, Nielsen Norman Group, March 19, 2000, https://www.nngroup.com/articles/why-you-only-need-to-test-with-5-users/.

[72] Skype, Zoom, Appear.in, and Google Hangouts are some free tools that come to mind.

[73] "How to Do Effective User Interviews?," Marc Abraham, April 20, 2014, https://marcabraham.com/2014/04/20/how-to-do-effective-user-interviews/.

[74] "Book Review: 'Lean UX,'" Marc Abraham, April 5, 2013, https://marcabraham.com/2013/04/05/book-review-lean-ux/.

generating true customer insights because you're leading the user in a certain direction, giving him or her the idea that there's a specific response that you're looking for.

3. **Keep it open-ended.** I've learned that it's better to leave the questions fairly open-ended and to try to avoid questions that can be answered with a simple yes or no. Better questions are ones that encourage users to explain their thinking or experiences. For example, "What about this landing page do you like? What don't you like? How do you typically find out about new music?" As part of the introduction to the session, I always explain to users that this isn't an exam and that there aren't any right or wrong answers.

4. **Avoid "Would you like this Ferrari?" type of questions.** My experience is that when you test a prototype or a new product with users, they are almost all likely to answer yes when you ask them whether they would buy or use this product. Thus it is a redundant question, and the answers are unlikely to tell you very much. No one can (accurately) predict future behaviour, and there are so many factors that will influence *actual* product usage that asking *would* questions will provide you with fairly meaningless insights in return. I have heard a good number of war stories where product people have made the mistake of thinking that their product would be a great success purely based on people saying during interviews that they *would* buy it.

5. **Combine user interviews with live prototypes.** Ideally, I prefer doing user interviews in conjunction with people actually using the product, even if it's still in its most minimal state. Whether a product is being used in beta or has been launched fully, tracking usage data will only help you to learn so much. User interviews provide a great way to find out more about the why behind the analytics data you can track.

6. **Listen, reflect, and probe.** Listen and be silent. These things are easier said than done when you are a passionate and opinionated product person, but they are vital when conducting user interviews. When I explain the purpose and format of the interview to users, I tend to warn them that I might not always respond (immediately) to their questions and that I will at times ask them to think out loud. This might sound a bit forced and unnatural, but understanding users' thought processes, considerations, or steps that they go through can be really insightful. UX people like Grace Ng,[75] Adrian

---

[75] "Quick Tips for Effective Customer Interviews," Grace Ng, accessed February 3, 2018, http://uxceo.com/post/80877539095/quick-tips-for-effective-customer-interviews.

Howard,[76] and Michael Hawley[77] have written some practical pointers on how to best paraphrase users and to ask why, what, when, or how questions to probe further.

The following are key product questions that user interviews (or other product discovery techniques) can help to address:[78]

- Do you understand who your users really are?
- How are users using your product?
- Can users figure out how to use your product? Where do they stumble?
- Why do users use your product?
- What do users like about your product?
- What do users want added to or changed in your product?

Here are some practical things to consider when preparing and running customer interviews:

When approaching customers to participate:

- **Think of the users you'd like to engage with.** Whether you use a recruitment agency like UK-based Indiefield or AnswerLab in the United States, a site like Ethnio, or if you recruit people yourself, it's important to have a clear idea of the target persona(s) you'd like to interact with.
- **Include the purpose, location, and duration of the interview session.** Inform the customer up-front of the nature of the session and its expected duration, and provide the details of the place where the interview will take place.
- **If you're offering users an incentive, outline the details.** I typically include details on the relevant incentive in the initial email (for example, an Amazon.com voucher).
- **Provide users with a range of dates and time slots to choose from.** There are tools that automate the process of scheduling slots, but you can always use a simple spreadsheet to keep track of available dates and time slots.

Preparing the questions and the room:

---

[76] "Effective Customer Interviewing," Adrian Howard, June 6, 2013, https://www.slideshare.net/adrianh/leanux-effectivecustomerinterviewingga20130606.

[77] "Preparing for User Research Interviews: Seven Things to Remember," Michael Hawley, UX Matters, July 7, 2008, http://www.uxmatters.com/mt/archives/2008/07/preparing-for-user-research-interviews-seven-things-to-remember.php.

[78] Cagan, *Inspired*, chapter 16.

- **Start with your desired learning outcomes.** I typically start drafting the desired learning outcomes first, before creating the interview outline. A good example of a learning outcome is "to understand how people currently solve this problem" or "to learn what customers like or dislike about our competitors." Having the learning outcomes of the interview clear in your head will help you create the interview outline and ensure you ask the right questions.
- **Create a high-level interview outline.** This is not a detailed script. This outline should provide you with a guide and reference point to use throughout the sessions. For example, an outline can contain any of the following elements: (1) interview objectives; (2) interview topics, themes, or scenarios that you want to cover; and (3) some initial questions or tasks related to each part of the interview (again, these don't have to be very detailed, but they should help to get the conversation going).
- **Create a user consent form.** The main purpose of this document is to ensure that the user is happy with you recording the session and using the data from the interview for internal purposes only.
- **Get a tape recorder and/or camera.** Use your phone or tape recorder to record the session. This not only helps you listen to the interview in full but also means you don't spend the entire session taking notes. Instead, you can focus on listening.
- **Get a comfortable chair and a drink.** I know it sounds obvious, but do make sure the user feels comfortable in the room or location where you're conducting the interview.
- **Don't create a tribunal setting.** Especially if you have two people conducting the interview (such as one person asking questions and one taking notes), it's important to avoid create a setting where the user feels that he or she is being interviewed for a job or grilled as part of an exam.

Facilitating the session:

- **Do at least one trial run.** I've learned the importance of doing at least one trial run of your user interview or your usability test. This will give you the opportunity to iron out any kinks or detect any questions or tasks that don't make sense to the user.
- **Prepare one other person.** Ideally, I like facilitating these sessions with one other person. This person can ask the user questions, take notes, or simply observe. I find this a great way to involve other people within the organisation (such as engineers or marketing people).

- **Introduce the interview session.** Again, this is a bit of a no-brainer, but it's nevertheless very important to explain to the user the nature of the session and the things you're hoping to learn and to ensure that the user feels comfortable asking *you* questions or seeking clarification.

7. Learning by Directly Observing Customers

It's about catching customers in the act, and providing highly relevant and highly contextual information.

—Paul Maritz, chair of Pivotal

One of the main benefits of simply observing customers is that you do not have to worry about asking leading questions or guiding customers down a certain path. Instead, you will watch customers using your (or a competitor's) product, ideally in their natural environment.

Accounting software company Intuit has been running an extensive customer programme since the company was founded in 1983.[79] Intuit employees spend time with their customers at their offices or homes to observe them whilst they are using Intuit's software products. This will, for example, give them an idea of how often customers are interrupted whilst they are doing their payroll or taxes.

In addition, Intuit employees talk to customers about their businesses and daily activities to get more context around customers and their needs or problems.[80] (See fig. 3.3.)

---

[79] "Intuit's CFO Wants to Follow You Home and Watch You Work," James Kosur, Business Insider, December 16, 2015, http://uk.businessinsider.com/intuits-cfo-wants-to-follow-you-home-and-watch-you-work-2015-12.
[80] "The Intuit Follow-Me-Home Program," Bryan Tritt, Intuit, accessed February 3, 2018, https://www.firmofthefuture.com/content/accounting-software-improvement-the-follow-me-home-program/.

Figure 3.3. Companies like Bang & Olufsen and Intuit use a follow-me-home approach to observe customers in their natural habitats.

High-end TV manufacturer Bang & Olufsen follow a similar approach, whereby researchers watch TV together with their customers in their own homes.[81] There are several common observation methods to consider, depending on the insights you are looking to gain from customers:

- **Field observation:** This means doing customer research in the field. For example, if you want to observe customers whilst they are shopping, the supermarket is your field. Do shoppers browse what is on the stacks, or do they know exactly what they are going for? Do they put things back on the shelves? You can observe and take notes, perhaps complemented by asking customers some questions.[82]
- **Contextual enquiry:** Although field observation is typically more informal, the contextual enquiry approach is a bit more structured. You identify

[81] "Adapt and Change," Bang & Olufsen, accessed February 3, 2018, http://blog.bang-olufsen.com/en/adapt-and-change.

[82] "Field Studies Done Right: Fast and Observational," Jakob Nielsen, Nielsen Norman Group, January 20, 2002, https://www.nngroup.com/articles/field-studies-done-right-fast-and-observational/.

appropriate users, schedule visits, carry out these visits, and then analyse what you have found and use it to design and build your product. It is about learning users' tasks, behaviours, values, and concerns.

- **Fly on the wall:** The fly-on-the-wall technique means you are observing without interacting with customers to avoid potential bias.[83] You observe exactly what you see and hear without asking the customer any questions. The risk with this approach is that you do not develop customer empathy or fully understand the context behind the things you are observing.
- **Shadowing:** By shadowing a customer intimately, you create a fuller picture of the customer, an insider's view. For example, I used to look over the shoulders of e-commerce sellers whilst they were managing their sales and stock levels online. That way, I learned not only about customer behaviours but also about their moods, facial expressions, and body language.

Key Takeaways

Understanding your customers is a critical aspect of being a product manager. It is easy to make assumptions about customers and their needs, but having real insight is invaluable, as it helps to ensure you are building a product that people want.

1. **Customer learning isn't a one-off.** Learning from customers is a continuous activity, and you are likely to learn different things at various stages of the product life cycle.
2. **Identify your customers first.** Before validating products or features with customers, it is important to first understand who your customers are. Such tools as empathy mapping help to capture and communicate your understanding of the customer persona.
3. **Keep customer research simple.** Customer research does not have to be expensive or time-consuming. Conducting customer interviews or observations is relatively straightforward. They are typically not hard to organise or carry out, and they will provide valuable customer insights to feed back into the product life cycle.

How to Apply These Takeaways

- **Schedule customer research during each development sprint.** Carving out time for customer research as part of each development sprint or

---

[83] "Fly-on-the-Wall Observation," Ellie Harmon, accessed February 3, 2018, http://ellieharmon.com/wp-content/uploads/UDM-Fly-on-the-Wall.pdf.

iteration is an effective way to get into the discipline of engaging with customers continuously. You can thus use customer research to test what you have built or to do some discovery for something you are looking the build in the next sprint.

- **Decide on segmentation criteria first to identify your customers.** Wading through reams of customer data in order to determine your customers' profiles can be very painful (and still not give you a better feel for who your customers are). As an alternative, I suggest selecting several customer segmentation criteria up-front and using these consistently to decide on customer profiles. For example, you could use set demographic criteria, such as age and occupation, to identify who your customers are.

- **Only plan your customer research once you have determined your learning outcomes.** Especially if you are relatively new to the different customer research techniques available, I strongly recommend that you define your desired customer learning outcomes first. These will depend largely on the stage of your product or business; if your product is completely new, you will want to learn different things from customers compared to when you have just refined an existing product. Establishing these learning outcomes will influence which research method is most appropriate. For example, if you wish to test the usability of a product, then a task-based interview could be a great fit. In contrast, if you are looking to validate customer problems, then direct observation might be more effective.

4
How to Get Started with Managing a Product

Goal

To learn where and how to get started with your product, whether it's an existing product or a product idea.

Related Tools and Techniques to Consider

- Create and communicate a **product vision** for your product, providing a clear direction for your product and concentrating on solving a customer problem.
- Be able to **tell a story** about your product, even if it does not exist yet.
- Conduct **market and trend analysis** to understand how to best position and differentiate your product.
- **Assess opportunities** to make sure you are focussing your efforts on the right problem(s) to solve.
- Determine measurable **assumptions and hypotheses** that you can validate with customers.
- Create a rapid **prototype** to test your initial assumptions quickly.
- Create a **minimum viable product (MVP)** to test your riskiest assumptions and hypotheses whilst delivering customer value.
- Use a simple **checklist** for the build and launch of your MVP.
- Decide whether to **pivot or persevere** with your product.

Introduction

It's better to build something that a small number of users love, than a large number of users like.
—Sam Altman, president of Y Combinator

It can be pretty daunting to start managing a product, whether the product already exists or is just an idea. With existing products, typically there tend to be a million and one things you could be doing with the product. Equally, if a product idea exists only on paper or in someone's head, there can also be a million and one things you could be doing with the product.

This raises the question of how you as a product manager can best make sure that you are building the right product (and for the right audience). In this chapter, we will look at how to provide direction for the product, starting with the product vision to deciding whether to stick with the product or to change direction.

1. Creating a Product Vision

Build the best product, cause no unnecessary harm, use business to inspire and implement solutions to the environmental crisis.

—Patagonia vision statement[84]

The main function of a product vision is to provide direction for a business, a product, or a service, concentrating on solving a question or problem—either from a customer or business perspective or both. As tempting as it is to jump straight into a product idea or to create features, a central product vision is where you need to start as a product manager. Everything else flows from there: product strategy, road map, problem statements, product discovery, prioritisation, and even your first prototypes.

Product Vision Statements

SpaceX was founded under the belief that a future where humanity is out exploring the stars is fundamentally more exciting than one where we are not. Today SpaceX is actively developing the technologies to make this possible, with the ultimate goal of enabling human life on Mars.

—SpaceX vision statement[85]

So-called product vision statements can be quite lofty and aspirational and thus indicate a more global type of goal—for example, "to provide clean and affordable energy for all households" or "to deliver organic food directly from the farm to your doorstep." The way in which one executes a vision is likely to evolve, but the overarching vision typically remains unchanged. (We will look at this more closely at the end of this chapter, when I discuss whether to pivot or persevere.)

For example, the long-form product vision statement for Mozilla Firefox reads as follows: "Discover, experience and connect with apps, websites and people on your own terms, everywhere." The tactics and solutions Mozilla implements to

---

[84] "Patagonia's Mission Statement," Patagonia, accessed February 3, 2018, http://www.patagonia.com/company-info.html.
[85] "Mission Management," SpaceX, accessed February 1, 2018, http://www.spacex.com/careers/position/213513.

achieve this vision are likely to evolve, but the overarching vision has remained unchanged for a good couple of years now.[86] The product vision statement for Firefox comes in two forms. The complete statement reads as follows: "Discover, experience and connect with apps, websites and people on your own terms, everywhere." The shorter version omits important parts but will be a more effective shorthand as the things it omits become implicit in everything we do: "Discover, experience and connect on your own terms."

Let's be clear: a product vision is not a strategy, nor is it a plan to achieve business or user goals. In my view, "We aim to deliver organic food to your doorstep by offering vegetables packaged in open crates and transported in specially created lorries" is not a vision. It is a strategy of how to best achieve a vision.

As I mentioned earlier, the product vision provides direction and a framework to make decisions against. A good product vision fits with company values. A good example is IKEA, where low prices form a core part of its overarching vision statement: "At IKEA our vision is to create a better everyday life for the many people. Our business idea supports this vision by offering a wide range of well-designed, functional home furnishing products at prices so low that as many people as possible will be able to afford them."[87]
From a product development perspective, this means that the price tag is the first thing that needs to be designed when creating a new IKEA product: "We feel good design combines form, function, quality, sustainability at a low price. We call it 'Democratic Design'—we believe good home furnishing is for everyone."[88]

[86] "Vision Statement," Firefox, accessed June 30, 2011,
https://wiki.mozilla.org/Firefox/VisionStatement#Product_vision_statement.
[87] "This Is IKEA," IKEA, accessed February 3, 2018, http://www.ikea.com/gb/en/this-is-ikea/.
[88] "Democratic Design," IKEA, accessed February 3, 2018, http://www.ikea.com/gb/en/this-is-ikea/democratic-design-en-gb/.

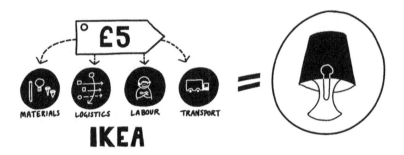

Figure 4.1. IKEA's Democratic Design vision

Characteristics of a Good Product Vision

First and foremost, a strong product vision must be clear and concise. However, there are several characteristics of a good product vision to consider beyond that:[89]

- It communicates the ultimate purpose for providing the product.
- It aligns with the company values.
- It envisages where the product will be in three years' time.
- It takes into account the consumer's needs.
- It's short and sweet.
- It's motivating.
- It can be used for decision making.

---

[89] "Learning about Creating a Good Product Vision," Marc Abraham, September 11, 2012, https://marcabraham.com/2012/09/11/learning-about-creating-a-good-product-vision/; "My Product Management Toolkit (1)—Product Vision," Marc Abraham, January 8, 2016, https://marcabraham.com/2016/01/08/my-product-management-toolkit-1-product-vision/.

How to Determine a Product Vision

Product vision statements have the biggest chance of success—that is, becoming a living and widely shared notion—if a lot of people inside and outside the organisation buy into it. A visioning workshop is a great way to make the creation of a product vision a collaborative process.

As a product manager, you play a pivotal role in the formulation of product vision and therefore in leading the visioning workshop. These are some of the key aspects to take into account when preparing for and facilitating a product-visioning workshop:[90]

- **Plan your goals.** Get buy-in for the vision early on from a range of internal and/or external stakeholders and leverage the knowledge of the group to come to an agreed product vision.
- **Have a rough idea of the vision beforehand.** As a product person, it's important to already have an idea of what the initial product vision and direction should look like. This will help in facilitating the workshop.
- **Listen, but don't make weak compromises.** Especially when you're doing a visioning workshop with a large group of stakeholders, it's important to listen to the different viewpoints but not to make weak compromises on the vision just to keep everybody in the room happy.
- **Consider stages of market maturity.** What stage is your target market at?[91] What is the competition like, and what are their differentiators? What are the needs of your market segment?

A good few years ago, I developed a product called HipHopListings, or HHL, a mobile app that presented hip-hop fans with listings of hip-hop shows and releases.[92] I created a long version of the vision statement for my product:

> HipHopListings is a mobile app for UK hip-hop fans who want to be kept up-to-date on hip-hop events across the United Kingdom as well as hip-hop releases. Our app lets users find out about hip-hop shows or releases by artists they might not even have heard about but will be triggered to go and

---

[90] "Creating a Shared Vision That Works," Alan Colville, *UX Magazine*, March 28, 2012, http://uxmag.com/articles/creating-a-shared-vision-that-works.
[91] "Market Maturity," Jared M. Spool, User Interface Engineering, January 1, 1997, https://articles.uie.com/market_maturity/.
[92] "Developing My Own Product—Creating a Product Vision," Marc Abraham, March 9, 2013, https://marcabraham.com/2013/03/09/developing-my-own-product-creating-a-product-vision/.

check out. Our app goes beyond specific artists you wish to track and gives you a complete overview of upcoming hip-hop shows and releases, making sure you have full access to what's going on and letting you filter this information by location or date.

Looking back on this statement, I can now see how the lion's share of it is about what the app *does* as opposed to a higher-level direction for the product. When I reflect on the shorter versions of the vision statement that I created at the time, I feel that some of these statements do more justice to what I was looking to achieve with my product:

- A great overview of hip-hop gigs and releases at your fingertips.
- Enabling hip-hop fans to access gig and release information where and when they like.
- A comprehensive list that lets users filter shows by location and date.
- A single source for all hip-hop concert and release information.
- An app that doesn't track artists but that tracks all the releases and shows in the genre you're passionate about.

2. Telling a Product Story

In order to resist the temptation to jump straightaway into designing and building your product, I strongly recommend thinking about your product story first. Figuring out the story you want to tell with your product is not just a fun exercise; a good story can help unlock important questions:

- **Who are the main characters in the story?** Which customers are you targeting with the product? What do these customers look like and why? Who are the key people within the business who are pivotal for the product's success? What will their roles be?
- **What is the story's hook? What will draw people to the product?** When telling a story, you can use a hook to kick off a narrative, or you can refer to the hook throughout the story.[93] A hook can be an underlying theme or worldview that readers or listeners can relate to and that will help in retaining people's attention. For example, when I created the HipHopListings app, the hook was all about people wanting to find out

---

[93] "My Product Management Toolkit (15): Storytelling," Marc Abraham, November 2, 2016, https://marcabraham.com/2016/11/02/my-product-management-toolkit-15-storytelling/.

about the next great hip-hop show in a town near them, not knowing when and where the show was going to take place.

- **Where does the story begin and end?** Over the years, I have become a great fan of the internal press release technique that product people within Amazon.com use when starting to think about a new product.[94] At Amazon, the product development process starts with a product manager writing an internal press release in which the finished product is announced. The press release is written from the customer's perspective, explaining how the product solves the customer's problem and how it is different from products already in the market. Like any story that begins with the end state, you can then start working backward to tell how the story unfolds and to think about issues, challenges, or successes along the way.

- **Are there any critical scenes or chapters in the story?** What are the specific outcomes that you want your customers to achieve through your product? Do you envisage specific iterations for your product? It helps to think about how you want your product to evolve, from a first release or minimum viable product into a product with all the necessary features that will solve customer problems.

Ian McAllister, former senior manager of product development at Amazon, discusses the company's approach to product development and product management:[95]

> For new initiatives a product manager at Amazon typically starts by writing an internal press release announcing the finished product. The target audience for the press release is the new/updated product's customers, which can be retail customers or internal users of a tool or technology. Internal press releases are centered around the customer problem, how current solutions (internal or external) fail, and how the new product will blow away existing solutions.

> If the benefits listed don't sound very interesting or exciting to customers, then perhaps they're not (and shouldn't be built). Instead, the product manager should keep iterating on the press release until they've come up

[94] "What Is Amazon's Approach to Product Development and Product Management?" Ian McAllister, May 18, 2012, https://www.quora.com/Amazon-company-What-is-Amazons-approach-to-product-development-and-product-management; "Product Management at Amazon—What Is It Like?" Marc Abraham, November 26, 2014, https://marcabraham.com/2014/11/26/product-management-at-amazon-what-is-it-like/.

[95] "What Is Amazon's Approach to Product Development and Product Management?" Ian McAllister, May 18, 2012, https://www.quora.com/Amazon-company-What-is-Amazons-approach-to-product-development-and-product-management.

with benefits that actually sound like benefits. Iterating on a press release is a lot less expensive than iterating on the product itself (and quicker!).

Here's an example outline for the press release:

- **Heading:** Name the product in a way the reader (your target customers) will understand.
- **Subheading:** Describe who the market for the product is and what benefit they get. One sentence only underneath the title.
- **Summary:** Give a summary of the product and the benefit. Assume the reader will not read anything else, so make this paragraph good.
- **Problem:** Describe the problem your product solves.
- **Solution:** Describe how your product elegantly solves the problem.
- **Quote from you:** A quote from a spokesperson in your company.
- **How to get started:** Describe how easy it is to get started.
- **Customer quote:** Provide a quote from a hypothetical customer that describes how they experienced the benefit.
- **Closing and call to action:** Wrap it up and give pointers on where the reader should go next.

If the press release is more than a page and a half, it is probably too long. Keep it simple: three to four sentences for most paragraphs. Cut out the fat. Don't make it into a spec. You can accompany the press release with a FAQ that answers all of the other business or execution questions so the press release can stay focussed on what the customer gets. My rule of thumb is that if the press release is hard to write, then the product is probably going to suck. Keep working at it until the outline for each paragraph flows.

The following is an example press release for a fictitious product:

How the new Leo Listening app makes note-taking easier than ever before

[17 January 2020]

A pen and a notebook are no longer needed to take great notes.

How often do we go to important meetings or conferences and write down tonnes of notes? When we then look back on the notes we have taken, we realise that most of our notes no longer mean anything to us, and we are no longer sure about what was decided or what we learned.

With the release of the Leo Listening app, available in iOS and Android, scenarios like the aforementioned will become things of the past. With the Listening app, you can now record a discussion or talk, and it will automatically give you all the notes from the session, both in plain text and in visual format.

"The idea for the Leo Listening app came up when I had been to an important sales meeting in which we made some critical decisions. When I looked at my notes after the meeting, the things I had jotted down no longer made any sense, and I couldn't remember the decisions we had made," explains Jack Rose, founder of Leo Listening. "When I started talking to other professionals, both at meetings and at events, I learned that note-taking was a common problem among a lot of people and therefore a problem worth solving."

The Listening app is underpinned by artificial technology and voice recognition to make sure that the app interprets everything that has been said correctly and converts it into a comprehensive story for the user. If you wish for the app to concentrate on specific words or phrases, you set these as preferences when assigning a task for Leo.

Just go to the Apple app store or the Google Play store, search for "Leo," and start taking notes!

3. Storyboarding: Creating a Story Together

I recently took part in a sketching session at a digital agency where we went spent a lot of time sketching user interfaces for Mobil without really understanding the underlying customer story first. This is where I have found the storyboarding technique introduced by Sarah Doody, a well-known UX design and product consultant, to be most helpful.[96]

Doody's key point is that "before presenting designs, you should first formulate the story you're telling through the designs," and storyboards offer an easy way of

---

[96] "3 Ways Storytelling Can Improve Your Product Development Process," Sarah Doody, August 12, 2015, http://www.sarahdoody.com/3-ways-storytelling-can-improve-your-product-development-process/.

doing so. In the sketching workshop, I felt we could have benefitted from fully understanding the customer and their current interactions first.

There are five key steps to cover in your storyboarding exercise:

1. Identify the **problem**.
2. Establish the **characters**.
3. Write out the **moments**.
4. Overlay moments with **emotions, actions, and thoughts**.
5. Sketch out each **scene** until the end of the story.

It can be tricky to get started on the "problem" part of Doody's storyboarding exercise. This is where the situation-complication-resolution framework can help. It's a useful tool to think about your story in a more structured manner.

4. Situation-Complication-Resolution Framework

Instead of creating a more traditional story, the situation-complication-resolution framework offers another way to tell a story about your product. Introduced in 2014 by Dave McKinsey, this framework can help to take listeners or readers along on the journey of your product and its (target) customers.[97] One of the things I like about this framework is that you don't have to apply it in a linear fashion.

- **Start with the situation.** You can start with the situation and then follow with the complication and end with the resolution. You'll thus take the reader or listener on a fairly linear journey, painting a picture of the current state, building tension and urgency through the complication, and bringing closure through the resolution.
- **Start with the complication.** This approach follows a nonlinear narrative form by beginning in the middle of the action and providing context after gaining the audience's interest. In cases where you want to make sure that your audience is fully engaged right from the beginning, it can pay off to start with the complication.
- **Start with the resolution.** Starting with the proposed solution first can be helpful in scenarios when the audience is short of time or very keen to hear the outcome. I've found that the risk with this approach is that in pitch situations you might not get a chance to explain the context around your

---

[97] Dave McKinsey, *Strategic Storytelling: How to Create Persuasive Business Presentations* (North Charleston, SC: CreateSpace, 2014).

solution (situation and complication), as the audience is keen to hash out the proposed solution or to talk through versions of it.

Let's assume that we want to tell the story of our fictitious new product called Zone Out, which enables people to let their coworkers know when they are in the zone and therefore don't want to be disturbed.

Let's look at some examples of how to apply the situation-complication-resolution framework (non)linearly to the story of Zone Out.

Start with the situation.
This is the story of Pete, who works at a top-tier consulting firm. Each time Pete wants to spend some thinking time at his desk, a colleague who wants to pick his brain or just chat about last night's basketball results distracts him.

Not only does this keep Pete from his thinking time but also he then finds it hard to go back into what he was doing and often needs to start all over again. He thus loses a lot of precious time and effort.

Since Pete has started using Zone Out, none of his colleagues have disturbed him during his designated thinking time. By Pete simply clicking on the Zone Out light that he has attached to his laptop screen, his coworkers can now see from a distance that Pete does not want to be disturbed. As soon as Pete has switched off the Zone Out light, his colleagues know that Pete is available again.

Start with the resolution.
Since Pete has started using Zone Out, none of his colleagues have disturbed him during his designated thinking time. By Pete simply clicking on the Zone Out light that he has attached to his laptop screen, his coworkers can now see from a distance that Pete does not want to be disturbed. As soon as Pete has switched off the Zone Out light, his colleagues know that Pete is available again.

Before using Zone Out, Pete was interrupted nonstop by his colleagues. Whenever Pete wanted to spend some thinking time at his desk, a colleague who wanted to pick his brain or just chat about last night's basketball results distracted him.

Not only did this keep Pete from his thinking time but also he found it hard to go back into what he was doing and often needed to start all over again. He thus lost a lot of precious time and effort.

Start with the complication.
Whenever Pete, who works at a top-tier consulting firm, gets distracted by a colleague, he finds it hard to go back into what he was doing and often needs to start all over again. He thus loses a lot of precious time and effort.

Each time Pete wants to spend some thinking time at his desk, a colleague who wants to pick his brain or just chat about last night's basketball results distracts him.

Since Pete has started using Zone Out, none of his colleagues have disturbed him during his designated thinking time. By Pete simply clicking on the Zone Out light that he has attached to his laptop screen, his coworkers can now see from a distance that Pete does not want to be disturbed. As soon as Pete has switched off the Zone Out light, his colleagues know that Pete is available again.

In conclusion, storytelling can really start to manage a product. The key thing is to think carefully about the story you would like to tell and to structure it accordingly.

5. Watching and Understanding Trends

Studying trends offers another good starting point for managing a product. As a product manager, I know how easy it can be to get trapped in the everyday and to lose sight of what the future could bring. We tend to get immersed in the more tactical day-to-day stuff and to forget about the bigger picture. There also seems to be a daily avalanche of new technology developments and market trends, and it can be tempting to act on the latest trend out of sheer fear of missing out.[98]

This raises the question of how you know whether a certain trend is worth following up on. The Trend Canvas, developed by a company called TrendWatching, is a useful tool that helps identify and assess trends. (See fig. 4.2.)

---

[98] "Trend-Driven Innovation for Product Managers—with Max Luthy," Chad McAllister, August 25, 2016, https://www.linkedin.com/pulse/trend-driven-innovation-product-managers-max-luthy-mcallister-phd/.

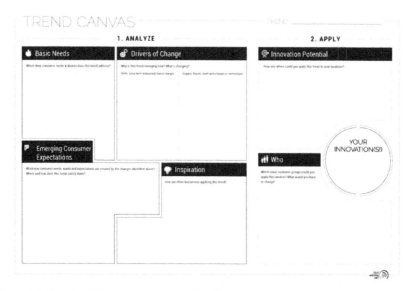

Figure 4.2. The Trend Canvas by TrendWatching[99]

The Trend Canvas distinguishes between the analyse and the apply stages. During the analyse stage, you assess a trend and its underlying drivers. What are the basic consumer needs a trend is serving and why? What kinds of change is this trend driving and why? In contrast, during the apply stage, you'll look at ways in which you and your business can best tap into a trend and who would benefit from it.

I have found the Trend Canvas to be very useful when exploring and assessing trends. The thing I like most about this framework is that it forces you to think about the customer and how he or she is influenced by a particular trend.

The trend of electric cars is a good one to analyse and apply. (See fig. 4.3.)

Analyse Trends

1. **Basic needs: What deep consumer needs and desires does this trend address?** I have not spoken to many electric car owners yet, but the ones I

---

[99] "Consumer Trend Canvas," TrendWatching, accessed February 3, 2018, http://trendwatching.com/x/wp-content/uploads/2014/05/2014-05-CONSUMER-TREND-CANVAS1.pdf.

have spoken to mention environmental consciousness and cost saving as the basic needs that drove their purchase of an electric car. The experts at TrendWatching mention some other typical types of basic needs worth considering as part of your analysis, including social status, self-improvement, entertainment, excitement, connection, security, identity, relevance, social interaction, creativity, fairness, honesty, freedom, recognition, simplicity, and transparency.[100]

2. **Drivers of change: Why is this trend emerging now? What's changing?** To analyse the drivers of change, it is worth looking at shifts and triggers. Shifts are the long-term, macro changes that often take years or decades to fully materialise. For example, a rapidly growing global middle class and increasing scarcity of oil are significant drivers of the appeal of electric cars.[101] Triggers are the more immediate changes that drive the emergence of a consumer trend. These can include specific technologies, political events, economic shocks, and environmental incidents. I feel that recent improvements to both the technology and the infrastructure with regard to electric cars are important triggers.

3. **Emerging consumer expectations: What new consumer needs, wants, and expectations are created by the changes previously identified? Where and how does this trend satisfy them?** Purchasing expensive fuel for your car is no longer a given, and consumers are starting to become more aware of the cheaper and environmentally friendly alternative in electric cars.

4. **Inspiration: How are other businesses applying this trend?** When analysing a trend, a key part of the analysis involves looking at how incumbent businesses are applying a trend. For example, the Renault-Nissan alliance has thus far been the most successful when it comes to electric cars.[102] Learning about the why behind their success will help one's own trend analysis.

---

[100] Ibid.

[101] Jess Chen, Jennifer Todd, and Frankie Clogston, *Creating the Clean Energy Economy: Analysis of the Electric Vehicle Industry* (Washington, DC: International Economic Development Council, 2013).

[102] "10 Car Companies That Sell the Most Electric Vehicles," Eric Schaal, The Cheat Sheet, September 16, 2015, https://www.cheatsheet.com/automobiles/10-car-companies-that-sell-the-most-electric-vehicles.html/.

Figure 4.3. Electric cars are a good subject for trend analysis.

Apply Trends

1. **Innovation panel: How and where could you apply this trend to your business?** This is one of the crucial steps when exploring trends—asking yourself that all-important question of how can I best apply this trend to my business? For example, how does a specific trend fit with our current offering of products and services? Why (not)? It's similar to when you assess a product opportunity and go through several questions to look at the viability of a trend for your business:[103]

   - **Vision:** How will the deeper shifts underlying this trend shape your company's long-term vision?
   - **Business model:** Can you apply this trend to launch a new business venture or brand?
   - **Product/service/experience:** What new products and services could you create in light of this trend? How will you adapt your current products and services?

---

[103] "Consumer Trend Canvas," TrendWatching, accessed February 3, 2018, http://trendwatching.com/x/wp-content/uploads/2014/05/2014-05-CONSUMER-TREND-CANVAS1.pdf.

- **Campaign:** How can you incorporate this trend into your campaigns and show consumers you speak their language—that you get it?
2. **Who? Which (new) customer groups could you apply this trend to? What would you have to change?** How often do we forget to think properly about who this trend is for and why they benefit from it? Which demographic is this trend relevant for and why? For instance, with electric cars, one could think about middle-class families who are very cost- and environmentally conscious consumers.

6. Assessing Market Viability

Once you have a good understanding of your target market and applicable trends, the next step is to assess the *viability* of that market. Is there any money to be made in this market? How complex is it to enter the market, both from a technology and a regulatory point of view? Is it already saturated, or is there room for new players to enter?

Questions like these may sound somewhat crude, but this is ultimately what assessing market viability comes down to. Although I firmly believe that endless market research quickly becomes counterproductive and results in analysis paralysis, it is nevertheless important to understand the market you are entering into with your product.

I learned a lot from Christophe Gillet, vice president of product management at Vimeo, who shared some valuable pointers on aspects to explore when considering market viability.[104] I have added some of my own sample questions to illustrate Gillet's questions:

1. **Is there a market?** This should be the first validation. Is there a demand for my product or service? Which market void will our product help to fill and why? What are the characteristics of my target market?
2. **Is there viability within that market?** Once you've established that there's a potential market for your product, this doesn't automatically mean that the market is viable. For example, regulatory constraints can make it hard to launch or properly establish your product in a market.
3. **What is the total addressable market?** The total addressable market—or total available market—is all about the revenue opportunity available for a particular product or service. (See fig. 4.4.) A way to work out the total

---

[104] "Assessing Market Viability Is Product Management," Christophe Gillet, This Is Product Management, accessed February 3, 2018, https://www.thisisproductmanagement.com/episodes/assessing-market-viability/.

addressable market is to first define total market space and then to look at the percentage of the market that has already been served.

4. **Is there a problem to solve?** It is important to validate early and often whether there is an actual problem that your product or service is solving.[105]

5. **Understand prior failures (by competitors).** Looking at previous competitor attempts can be an easy thing to overlook. However, understanding who already tried to conquer your market of choice and whether they have been successful can help you avoid some pitfalls that others encountered before you.

6. **Talk to individual users.** This is almost a given if you're looking to validate whether there's a market and a problem to solve. Make sure that you sense check your market and problem assumptions with your target customers.[106]

7. **Have a strong mission statement and objectives of what you are looking to achieve.** Having a clear mission statement helps to articulate and communicate what it is you're looking to achieve and why. These mission statements are typically aspirational but should offer good insight into your aspirations for a particular market. The mission statement of Hilton Hotels is a good example in this respect: "To be the most hospitable company in the world—by creating heartfelt experiences for Guests, meaningful opportunities for Team Members, high value for Owners and a positive impact in our communities."[107]

8. **Develop business goals.** Having clear, measurable objectives in place to achieve in relation to a new market that you are considering is absolutely critical.[108] There is nothing worse than looking at new markets without a clear definition of what market success looks like and why.

9. **Determine how to get people to use your product.** I really liked how Christophe Gillet mentioned the need to think about a promotion and an adoption strategy. Too often I encounter a build-it-and-they-will-come mentality, which can be deadly if you are looking to enter new markets. Having a clear go-to-market strategy is almost just as important as developing a great product or service. What's the point of an awesome product that no one knows about or doesn't know where to get?

[105] "My Product Management Toolkit (5): Assumptions and Hypotheses," Marc Abraham, February 18, 2016, https://marcabraham.com/2016/02/18/my-product-management-toolkit-5-assumptions-and-hypotheses/.

[106] "Interviewing Customers to Explore Problems and Solutions," Marc Abraham, June 24, 2015, https://marcabraham.com/2015/06/24/interviewing-customers-to-explore-problems-and-solutions/.

[107] "Vision, Mission, and Values," Hilton Worldwide, accessed February 3, 2018, http://hiltonworldwide.com/about/mission/.

[108] "My Product Management Toolkit (3)—Goal Setting," Marc Abraham, January 28, 2016, https://marcabraham.com/2016/01/28/my-product-management-toolkit-3-goal-setting/.

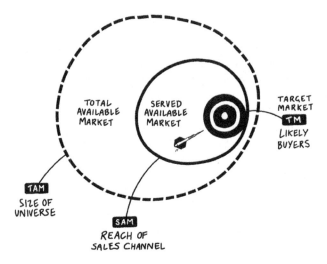

Figure 4.4. Defining the target market for your product

7. Assessing Opportunities

Don't be surprised if exploring trends and assessing market viability presents you with an abundance of product opportunities to choose from. This brings us to the often-dreaded "p" word: prioritisation.

A lot of product managers have a love-hate relationship with prioritisation, constantly having to choose between ideas and making tough trade-off decisions. Whichever way you look at it, prioritisation is part and parcel of our job as product managers. Before you prioritise a specific solution, I recommend that you always start by assessing whether the problem is worth solving in the first place.

I am now going to focus on assessing the opportunity related to solving a particular problem. Is it worthwhile to solve the problem? Why (not)? Has the problem already been solved? If so, by whom and how? A simple opportunity assessment or business case can be very effective in helping to decide whether to create a product.

What Is a Product Opportunity Assessment?

A product opportunity statement is a simple template invented by Marty Cagan that is meant to help people concentrate on the right opportunities.[109] How do you know which opportunities to focus on and which ones to discard? How do you prioritise between great-sounding product idea A and great-sounding product idea B? What are the grounds on which you base such a—typically difficult—decision?

Cagan's product opportunity assessment helps us work through these thorny questions in a systematic and structured manner:

1. Exactly what problem will this solve? (Value proposition)
2. For whom do we solve that problem? (Target market)
3. How big is the opportunity? (Market size)
4. What alternatives are out there? (Competitive landscape)
5. Why are we best suited to pursue this? (Our differentiator)
6. Why now? (Market window)
7. How will we get this product to market? (Go-to-market strategy)
8. How will we measure success/make money from this product? (Metrics/revenue strategy)
9. What factors are critical to success? (Solution requirements)
10. Given the previous, what's the recommendation? (Go or no-go)

This approach enables the comparison of product opportunities or ideas in an objective and like-for-like manner. Instead of going for the first solution to a problem that sounds right or seems cool, you are taking a step back and assessing several (competing) market or product opportunities, using the same questions or metrics to do an objective comparison.

Going through the process of assessing a product opportunity makes it easier to have focussed conversations about a product strategy or specific goals that you are looking to deliver on.

What a Product Opportunity Assessment Is Not

An opportunity assessment does not aim to provide a solution to a business or customer problem. In contrast, it helps answer the question of whether it is worthwhile to *solve* the problem in the first place. Another way to look at this is to

---

[109] Cagan, *Inspired.*

examine the *value* or *outcome* you are trying to provide to an individual customer or business.

When to Do a Product Opportunity Assessment

Too often I see business people or product managers jumping straight into what I call feature mode. They come up with a feature or solution instead of first looking at the problem to solve (and whether it is worth solving) or the specific business or customer outcome to achieve. In this regard I have learned a lot from Valve, a well-known gaming company, and from Tony Ulwick.[110, 111] Both Valve and Ulwick focus on outcomes instead of outputs. It is not about creating feature X. It is about the value that this or any feature generates for the customer and your business. Similar to creating a business case, a product opportunity assessment helps you and your stakeholders understand why a problem is worth solving (or why not) and the value it will generate once solved.

Another useful framework was created by my friends at Xing, a business-networking platform aimed at German-speaking users. This framework is called ACE and stands for assignment clarification exercise. (See fig. 4.5.) Similar to Marty Cagan's product opportunity assessment template, Xing's framework urges you to think about such aspects as context and outcome.

Especially in situations where you've got a lot of opportunities to choose from, assessing the opportunity using Cagan's questions helps you to compare opportunities or ideas objectively. Whether you create a full-fledged business case or use Cagan's template, the key is that you assess the problem you're thinking of solving, the competition, your target audience, and so forth. You are thus assessing the context around a problem, understanding whether it's a problem worth solving or prioritising.

---

[110] Valve, *Handbook for New Employees* (Bellevue, WA: Valve, 2012).
[111] Anthony W. Ulwick, *What Customers Want: Using Outcome-Driven Innovation to Create Breakthrough Products and Services* (New York: McGraw-Hill, 2005).

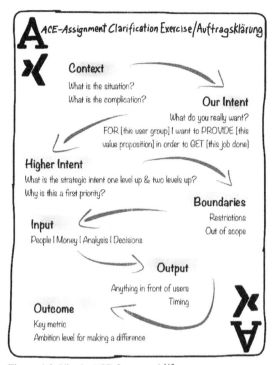

Figure 4.5. Xing's ACE framework[112]

8. Measurable Assumptions and Hypotheses

In chapter 3, we looked at problem statements to effectively capture customer problems to solve. Once you have defined and understood the problem(s) you are looking to solve, the next step is to validate ways to solve the problem. How do you know that you have solved a problem successfully?

I learned a lot in this respect from the Lean UX approach to things, as introduced by Jeff Gothelf and Josh Seiden.[113] The key point to Lean UX is the definition and validation of assumptions and hypotheses. This approach is ultimately about managing risks: customer risk, technology risk, or market risk. Instead of a single

---

[112] "Framework No 9: Auftragsklärung," Timm Richter, accessed February 3, 2018, http://produktfuehrung.de/framework-no-9-auftragsklarung/.
[113] Gothelf and Seiden, Lean UX.

big-bang product release, you constantly iterate and learn from actual customer usage of the product. As Gothelf explains, the goal is to "get customer feedback early and often."[114] He refers to this as "the velocity of learning."[115]

Assumptions

When thinking about problems and how to best solve them, we tend to make a lot of assumptions. This often happens almost automatically, without challenging the assumption too much. For example, we assume that our customers will use our product in a certain way or are happy to pay for it.

Another example comes from Alan Klement, principal at Idealized Innovation, who points out the flaws inherent in user stories based on personas. As we discussed in chapter 3, user personas are fictitious to begin with. Consequently, if we use these invalidated personas from which to derive user stories, our user stories won't be grounded in real user needs or behaviours. (See fig. 4.6.) We will have created one major assumption as a result.

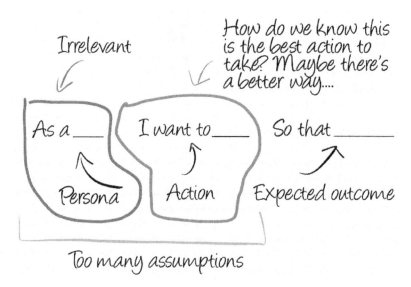

[114] "Jeff Gothelf and Lean UX," Marc Abraham, August 23, 2015, https://marcabraham.com/2015/08/23/jeff-gothelf-and-lean-ux/.
[115] "Optimizing Your Team's Velocity (of Learning)," Jeff Gothelf, Medium, May 8, 2017, https://medium.com/@jboogie/optimizing-your-teams-velocity-of-learning-700fd9ee10e4.

Figure 4.6. Alan Klement's views on personas that haven't been validated[116]

The biggest problem is not so much about the assumptions themselves but about (not) validating one's assumptions before designing a product or service. The Lean UX approach introduced by Gothelf and Seiden exposes assumptions from the start and offers a way to validate these assumptions early and often.

Hypotheses

Hypotheses help with testing your assumptions. A hypothesis statement is a more granular version of the original assumption and is formulated in such a way that you can test and measure specific desired *outcomes*:[117]

> We believe that
> [doing this]
> For [these people]
> Will achieve this [outcome].
> We will know this is true when
> [this market feedback].

You can use these hypothesis statements to test a specific product area or workflow. The key thing with assumptions and hypotheses is their focus on behavioural outcomes or changes, not just on the feature or solution you are looking to build.

The hypothesis needs to be measurable to be able to obtain the desired learnings. For example, "We know our assumption holds true if we see a ten percent increase in revenue as a result of the launch of the new product" or "We know we are on the right path if the average revenue per user increases by two percent within three months following the launch of the new feature."

It is also important to validate your riskiest assumptions first. I've benefited enormously from using simple prototypes to validate such risky assumptions as "This feature will solve my customer's problem" or "Customers will pay for this service" before committing lots of time, money, and effort to solving a problem.

[116] "Replacing the User Story with the Job Story," Alan Klement, Medium, November 12, 2013, https://jtbd.info/replacing-the-user-story-with-the-job-story-af7cdee10c27.
[117] "Lean UX + UX STRAT," Josh Seiden, September 10, 2013, https://www.slideshare.net/UXSTRAT/ux-strat-2013-josh-seiden-lean-ux-ux-strat.

This comes back to the build-measure-feedback loop we examined in chapter 2. As product people, we are constantly looking to find problems, hypothesise a solution, and iterate on the solution. (See fig. 4.7.)

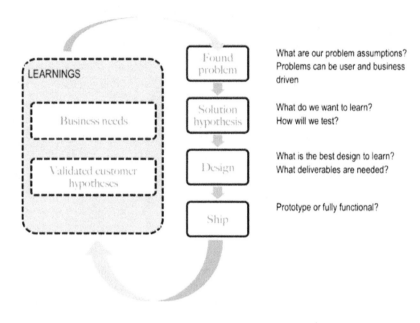

Figure 4.7. Maximilian Wambach's outline of hypothesis-driven UX design[118]

I have, however, seen some people fall into the trap of treating assumptions and hypotheses as absolute truths. The point of having assumptions and hypotheses is being transparent up-front about educated guesses, unknowns, or risks. In the next few sections, we will look at how to bring some of these risks forward and mitigate them.

9. (Rapid) Prototyping

When I come across companies that have not tested any prototypes with users before designing and building a product, my heart cannot help but sink a bit. Although I appreciate that you have to be careful with testing prototypes of certain

[118] "Hypothesis Driven UX Design," Maximilian Wambach, Medium, January 11, 2015, https://medium.theuxblog.com/hypotheses-driven-ux-design-c75fbf3ce7cc.

products—think pharmaceutical drugs—there are big risks associated with not testing a prototype version of a product before launching it. Prototypes come in all shapes and sizes, often referred to as low or high fidelity. (See the respective examples in fig. 4.8). The level of fidelity indicates how close the prototype comes to functioning as the real, usable product.

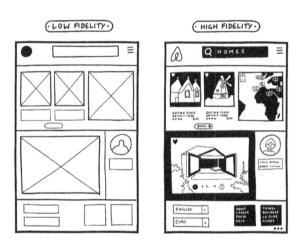

Figure 4.8. Prototypes come in all different ranges of fidelity.

Prototyping is at the core of experimentation; it provides a quick way to validate your assumptions with real users and to tackle key product risks early on in the process. It can be as simple as using a piece of paper with a sketch of a new feature for initial product validation. The main thing is that you use a prototype to mitigate risk by getting feedback early and often in the product (development) life cycle.

In their book *What Product Managers Need to Know about Rapid Prototyping*, Mike Fishbein and Josh Wexler argue that experimentation is a key part of the product manager's role.[119] As a result, the authors explain that "the product manager's primary role becomes enabling experimentation as a seamless capability. At the core of experimentation is rapid prototyping."

---

[119] Mike Fishbein and Josh Wexler, *What Product Managers Need to Know about Rapid Prototyping* (New York: Alpha UX, 2015).

In their book, Fishbein and Wexler provide some valuable tips in relation to doing prototypes:

- **Differentiate between generative and evaluative experiments.** The distinction between generative and evaluative experiments is an important one. Typically, new products or features will start with generative experiments—identifying and assessing customer pain points or problems. In contrast, evaluative experiments are used to evaluate different options for a product direction. You are evaluating several ways to resolve a customer pain point that you've established during a generative experiment. Rapid prototyping is critical during evaluative experiments because it will help you assess whether your product solution is viable.
- **Consider constraints when prototyping.** Using the words *prototyping* and *constraints* in one sentence might sound like a contradiction in terms, as you might think that prototype means having free rein. In contrast, it is important to pay attention to constraints when creating prototypes. Fishbein and Wexler suggest several important questions to ask before creating a prototype:[120]
  - What's my or my organisation's risk or threshold?
  - What's my capability given my current budget?
  - What's my organisation's domain of discretion?
  - Am I overconstraining?
- **Use a learning model to plot perception of value versus simulation of value.** Fishbein and Wexler describe the perception of value (PV) as "a conglomeration of metrics that together provide insight into comparative user feedback." In other words, the higher the PV, the better. Simulation of value (SV) shows how close the user is to actually experiencing value. Going back to my earlier example of a simple sketch on a piece of paper, this might generate a high PV because the user gets the value, but the SV is likely to be very low in comparison. It's fair to say that higher SV values will generate more reliable user learnings and insights, as the prototype delivers more concrete value to the user.
- **Plot goals and constraints.** Although we might be tempted to think that the sky's the limit when prototyping, it is important to think about goals and constraints when creating a prototype. A good example of a prototype-related constraint is risk threshold, which represents the minimum amount of

---

[120] Ibid., 19–21.

data you need to collect before your business gives the green light for a product. The goal element covers the why and perceived value of a product.

- **Don't forget about the story.** In addition to perception and simulation, Fishbein and Wexler also suggest looking at the story. The story dimension represents a continuum of the user's narrative and how he or she might interact with the value proposition of a product. The book talks about a so-called double-dip effect. This effect typically occurs when product managers succeed in unlocking the story element; when iteration cycles are so short that following positive experiment results, product teams can run another experiment to understand the why behind the initial results. The key point here is that when prototyping becomes a rapid process, product managers will be able to fully learn the narrative of their (target) users.

- **Balance simulation of value with iteration time and resources.** Fishbein and Wexler also address some of the trade-offs inherent in rapid prototyping. They point out that "prototyping lower simulations of value costs less and has shorter iteration cycles than prototyping higher simulations of value." However, the insights you typically get from lower simulations of value are likely to be less reliable and detailed compared to high simulations of value. The following are Fishbein and Wexler's pointers on how to manage these trade-offs:[121]

  - **Stay in scope.** It's not about creating beautiful designs for your prototype. The goal is to learn about the users and their interactions with a product's value proposition as early and often as possible. Staying in scope is therefore a key notion.

  - **Adapt the methodologies.** No (prototyping) methodology is set in stone. Instead, Fishbein and Wexler recommend understanding the high-level purpose of each prototyping step and then adapting it to your organisation.

  - **Select technology that supports your best practices.** When it comes to prototyping, there are a thousand and one tools to choose from. The important part is to make sure that prototyping is an efficient and waste-reducing mechanism for learning about users and validating new product concepts.

10. An MVP to Get Your Product off the Ground

The first time I heard the term *minimum viable product*, or MVP, was in February 2012. In a jam-packed London auditorium, I listened to Eric Ries, author of *The*

---

[121] Ibid., 54–5.

Lean Startup, talk about how to best run learning experiments.[122] Since then, I have come across MVPs in all shapes and sizes (including those products that I perceive to be MVP wannabes, but more about those later).

Whether you call it an MVP or an MLP (minimum loveable product[123]), it's all about learning about your products and their users as quickly as you can. Naturally, any learning is valuable, but in Ries's original definition, the MVP is primarily created to test your riskiest assumption(s) before deciding to invest a lot of money, people, time, and effort into building the new product.

Since then, other champions of the Lean movement, such as Ash Maurya, have come up with a narrower MVP definition: a minimum viable product is the smallest thing you can build that delivers customer value (and, as a bonus, captures some of the value back).[124]

Maurya's main rationale for this new, tighter definition is that under the initial definition by Ries, such things as customer interviews, teaser pages, and demos were considered products, which they clearly weren't (if you apply some of the criteria for what constitute a product as addressed in chapter 1). Instead, Maurya explains, an MVP should deliver some form of customer value instead of merely validating certain start-up assumptions.

I believe in both Ries and Maurya's viewpoints and try to combine each when creating MVPs. Firstly, I can see why some people prefer using the term *minimum loveable product* instead of *minimum viable product*. I have seen plenty of examples where the customer experience aspect of the product clearly had been neglected in favour of getting something out there to see if it sticks. If this is your approach, chances are that you will not get the validated learnings you are looking for.

Instead, customer experience should be considered as an integral part of your MVP. This doesn't mean that your product needs to have all the bells and whistles or the slickest user experience the world has ever seen. As long as the specific experiment you are launching has been thought through properly, is functional, and

---

[122] "Eric Ries and Learning How to Pivot (or Persevere)," Marc Abraham, February 22, 2012, https://marcabraham.com/2012/02/22/eric-ries-and-learning-how-to-pivot-or-persevere/.
[123] "How to Build a Minimum Loveable Product," Laurence McCahill, Medium, November 12, 2014, https://medium.com/the-happy-startup-school/beyond-mvp-10-steps-to-make-your-product-minimum-loveable-51800164ae0c.
[124] "What Is a Minimum Viable Product (MVP)," Ash Maurya, June 12, 2017, https://blog.leanstack.com/minimum-viable-product-mvp-7e280b0b9418.

is usable and reliable, you stand a much better chance of realising your desired learning outcomes. (See fig. 4.9.)

For instance, if the goal of your product is to get people from A to B, there is no point in releasing a bicycle that has one wheel missing, as people will not be able to use it. Instead, with the MVP approach, you start with the release of a scooter before you launch a bike with all the bells and whistles on it. In other words, your MVP needs to deliver value to the customer from day one.

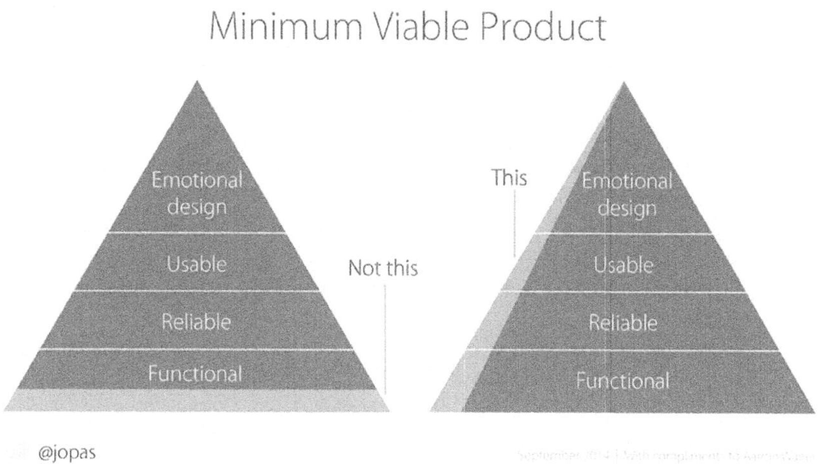

Minimum Viable Product

Figure 4.9. Aaron Walter's definition of a minimum viable product

Secondly, I *do* find thinking about the riskiest assumption a very helpful consideration and prioritisation tool when building an MVP. When you start building a new product from scratch, it's like a house of cards, with each card being an assumption. If you don't tackle the bottom row of cards first—that is, your riskiest assumptions—then ultimately all the cards will fold, and the house—that is, your product—will collapse. For instance, what is the point of building out a whole product if I'm not sure whether people will pay for it? Why would I build and launch several features if I haven't learned from my customers whether the product's core functionality benefits them?

Global accommodation service Airbnb is a great example of a successful MVP. The founders of Airbnb, Joe Gebbia and Brian Chesky, started with turning their apartment into a bed and breakfast for a few days and thus learned there was a market for offering people accommodation experiences.[125]

Just as much as an MVP is not an excuse for creating a subpar product or suboptimal experience, it is neither an alibi for the first phase of a product. A few years ago, I came across a company that spent a year building a product they referred to internally as an MVP. When I asked why this product was treated as an MVP, their product people explained that this was the first release and that they had a long list of additional features they could not include in the first release due to time constraints. The main problem I have with this kind of scenario is that it defeats the object of learning quickly and efficiently. Because I know how tempting it can be to fall into the trap of gold plating your MVP or going crazy with the number of initial features, I use the following safeguards to avoid this:[126]

1. **Identify customer needs and goals (problems).** Ask yourself, "Which problems are my MVP solving and for whom?"
2. **Keep it simple.** Keeping it simple does not mean creating a product that is a pain to use. Instead, the focus should be on trimming the fat—removing any functionality that is not critical to delivering value to the user and achieving desired learnings.
3. **Consider constraints.** For example, if you are designing an MVP for a mobile, there are several user interface constraints to take into account.

When I created my HipHopListings app, a mobile version of the eponymous Twitter feed I have been running since 2009,[127] I considered several things when deciding on the scope and design of my MVP:

1. **Identify customer needs and goals (problems).** The key user problems I was looking to address through my HHL app were twofold. Firstly, "How do I find out about upcoming hip-hop shows in my area and in time to get tickets?" Secondly, "How do I find out about upcoming hip-hop releases?" These assumptions were based on the feedback received from a large number of HHL followers on Twitter.
2. **Identify customer needs and goals (requirements).** In my brief to the developer, I translated the user problems just mentioned in the simplest way

---

[125] "How Airbnb Began," YouTube, published July 27, 2016, https://www.youtube.com/watch?v=GDBEsJGCJ_Y.
[126] "Developing My Own Product—Creating a Minimum Viable Product," Marc Abraham, May 22, 2013, https://marcabraham.com/2013/05/22/developing-my-own-product-creating-a-minimum-viable-product/.
[127] See https://twitter.com/hiphoplistings.

possible: (1) enable users to easily view upcoming shows and go to a third-party ticketing site, and (2) enable users to filter listings by area and date. (see figs. 4.10 and 4.11, respectively.) I also asked the developer to implement Google Analytics so that I could track users' actual behaviour and validate some of my assumptions.

3. **Keep it simple.** I decided to keep the design of the app as simple as possible at this stage. My main objective was to get the app approved by Apple first (which can be a real pain in itself) and then get people to use the app and comment on its functionality. My thinking was that I could always improve or add further functionality later on, provided I had successfully validated that users did indeed find the app valuable in terms of learning about hip-hop gigs and record releases.

4. **Identify customer needs and problems.** Based on previous feedback, I thought it would be good to add a very basic discovery element to the app: a simple Featured screen that users can turn to for curated shows and releases that I'd chosen to highlight. (See fig. 4.12.) I reckoned this feature would be relatively easy to get feedback on. Firstly, I would be able to monitor the number of views of this screen. Secondly, I felt this would be the kind of feature that would be easy to get qualitative user feedback on. I could use both feedback methods to validate one of my assumptions: making it as easy as possible for users to discover new shows and releases will be a powerful proposition for HHL's users.

5. **Consider constraints.** One of my personal goals was to learn more about designing for mobile. And learn I did. My original design went largely out the window as soon as I realised from user testing that Facebook's more traditional split-screen view would likely be easier to implement and for users to interact with. After all, I wanted a clean and simple interface, with no frills, and it looked like my original designs were too elaborate. Also, I quickly realised that I would have to update the app's content manually via a back-end process that had to be kept as simple and intuitive as possible. I spent a good chunk of my time thinking about the user flow involved in uploading, updating, and removing the app's content.

Despite my user research and what I felt was a sensible MVP approach, the HHL app did not achieve what I had hoped; about a hundred people downloaded the iOS version of the app, actual usage was minimal, and about half of the original cohort of users uninstalled the app after a month. Although I was disappointed with how the app was performing, I had to make a critical decision: pivot or persevere.

Figure 4.10. My initial design for a Shows screen to enable users to easily find out about upcoming shows and go to ticket sites.

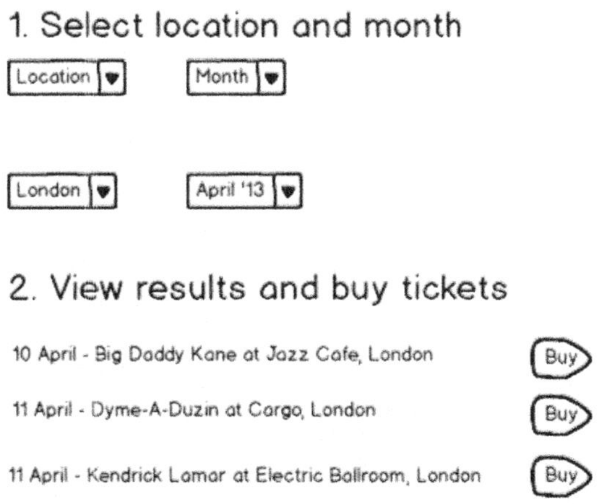

1. Select location and month

Location ▼   Month ▼

London ▼   April '13 ▼

2. View results and buy tickets

10 April - Big Daddy Kane at Jazz Cafe, London   〈Buy〉

11 April - Dyme-A-Duzin at Cargo, London   〈Buy〉

11 April - Kendrick Lamar at Electric Ballroom, London   〈Buy〉

Figure 4.11. My design for a filtering functionality to enable users to look only at shows in their area or by date.

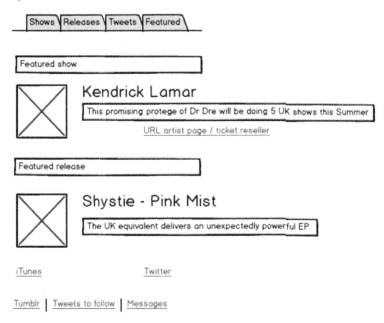

Shows \ Releases \ Tweets \ Featured \

Featured show

Kendrick Lamar

This promising protege of Dr Dre will be doing 5 UK shows this Summer

URL artist page / ticket reseller

Featured release

Shystie - Pink Mist

The UK equivalent delivers an unexpectedly powerful EP

iTunes   Twitter

Tumblr | Tweets to follow | Messages

Figure 4.12. My design for a Featured screen to highlight preselected shows and releases.

11. Pivot or Persevere

The first time I heard the term *pivot* was in the same jam-packed London auditorium I described in the previous section. It was Eric Ries who introduced the word *pivot* into strategy speak.[128] Since attending his talk in 2012, I have seen the term *pivot* being used and abused on more than one occasion.

When a business decides to pivot, it effectively changes its direction without totally abandoning its previous learnings or product vision. Instagram, the hugely successful photo-sharing app, began its life as Burbn, a check-in app that combined gaming and photos. (See fig. 4.13.) The people who built Burbn felt there was too much going on within the app and decided to trim the fat and focus solely on photography instead. There are plenty of examples out there of companies that changed direction successfully, such as PayPal and Pinterest.[129]

Pivoting is not about throwing prior learnings or products into the paper bin and starting afresh the following day with a totally blank piece of paper. The common denominator between companies that have pivoted successfully is that they stayed close to their underlying vision and reflected on previous learnings and experiences. In an ideal world, a company becomes very good at reducing time between pivots. This means that a business will decide early in the product life cycle (see chapter 1) whether to continue, iterate, or discontinue its product.

---

[128] "Eric Ries and Learning How to Pivot (or Persevere)," Marc Abraham, February 22, 2012, https://marcabraham.com/2012/02/22/eric-ries-and-learning-how-to-pivot-or-persevere/.

[129] "14 Famous Business Pivots," Jason Nazar, *Forbes*, October 8, 2013, https://www.forbes.com/sites/jasonnazar/2013/10/08/14-famous-business-pivots/.

Figure 4.13. A screenshot of Burbn, the predecessor to today's Instagram[130]

In regard to my HipHopListings app, I decided to drop the app altogether. Unfortunately, the uptake on the app and the user feedback did not warrant persevering with it. Looking back, applying the MVP approach taught me to start small and to constantly ask myself one question: "Should I pivot or persevere?"

Key Takeaways

It can often feel overwhelming to start thinking about a new product, and it is easy to get caught up in features and designs. Equally, some products have suffered from a tendency to just get something out there to see if it works. Your product can start off on a better footing if you take a step back and think about the product vision and story first.

1. **Have a clear product vision to offer direction.** It is important to have a clear vision for your product. A vision statement does not have to be very specific. A vision is not about the how of your product; it is much more about the what and why of your product or business. A good product vision is one that ties with the company's overall values.

---

[130] "Entrepreneurial Lessons from Instagram Co-Founder Kevin Nystrom," Kissmetrics, accessed February 3, 2018, https://blog.kissmetrics.com/kevin-systrom/.

2. **Recognise that product management is all about storytelling.** Thinking about your product before and whilst you are building it will help focus the mind on several key questions: Who is this product for? Who will pay for it and why? What are the hooks of my product? Answers to these kinds of questions are likely to form the heart of your product's story.
3. **Continuously identify and test assumptions.** As product managers, a key part of our role is to unearth assumptions, be it business or customer assumptions. Especially when you are starting with a new product, it is important to test the riskiest assumption first, as the success or failure of your product is likely to hinge on this riskiest assumption. Once validated, you can test the next riskiest assumption, and you will soon be immersed in a continuous learning cycle.

How to Apply These Takeaways

- **Start with a press release.** Before designing and building a product, start by writing a press release. This press release describes the successful launch of your product, including a description of its main customer benefits and some related customer quotes. You can then use this press release to work backward to start identifying key customer problems to solve and to prioritise features to build.
- **Use a prototype to learn quickly.** If you want to learn quickly about a new product proposition or simply to test the usability of a new feature, then it pays to do a rapid prototype. Remember, rapid prototypes aren't about delivering customer value but about managing risk—the risk of people not buying into your product or the product not working.
- **Use a minimum viable product (MVP) to validate your riskiest assumptions whilst delivering customer value.** Once you have determined the problems you want your product to solve and the associated assumptions and tested an initial prototype, then it's time to launch an MVP. Use your MVP both to deliver tangible customer value and to start validating your riskiest assumption(s). Delivering tangible value means that people can actually use the product to solve a problem, big or small, and validating assumptions means that you will generate learnings that you can then take into account when building subsequent product iterations.

5
Your Day-to-Day Product Management

Goal

To explore the different aspects of managing products throughout their life cycles and what this means for your day-to-day responsibilities.

Related Tools and Techniques to Consider

- Identify **common responsibilities** of day-to-day product management and why.
- Determine common outcomes of **day-to-day** product management.
- Understand why, as a product manager, it is important to **balance the day-to-day** with the forward-looking aspects of your product.
- **Prioritise,** make **trade-off decisions,** and **say no.**
- Know when to **retire** a product or feature.
- Use **data**—both quantitative and qualitative—to make product decisions.
- Write **user stories** and **acceptance scenarios** or acceptance criteria.
- **Reflect and improve** on your day-to-day product management.

Introduction

Excellent firms don't believe in excellence—only in constant improvement and constant change.

—Tom Peters

Although I fully appreciate that product management varies across organisations and products, I do believe there are several responsibilities that apply to product managers across the board. For example, prioritisation is part and parcel of product management as is using data to make product decisions. Regardless of the things you do as part of your day-to-day product management, I will stress in this chapter the importance of being able to step back from the day-to-day and to look forward.

1. Balance the Day-to-Day with Looking Forward

Once you achieve one goal, you should be looking forward to trying to build onto the next thing, and not just getting comfortable with what you're doing.

—LL Cool J

I remember working with another product manager once—let's call her Stacy—who explained to me how her main task was "to protect the long-term future of the product." In her experience, it was best to leave the designers and developers "to just get on with it." She believed it was best for product managers to get out of the way of who she referred to as the "doers." Instead, she focussed solely on creating and managing a product strategy, the road map, and stakeholder management.

My view of product management is altogether different. Contrary to Stacy's beliefs, I strongly feel that product managers should be closely involved in the day-to-day tasks and decisions associated with product ideas or improvements. This doesn't mean that product managers who look forward should be left out of the equation. In contrast, it is vital for the product manager to be more strategic.

Product managers should always have a keen eye on what's lying ahead for the product and why. Consequently, when outlining my approach, I tend to distinguish between the what and why, as well as the how, of product management. (See fig. 5.1.)

What and Why

As you might recall from chapter 2, understanding and communicating the why of your product is a quintessential element of product management. As soon as another person becomes involved with the product, it becomes critical for that person to understand the what and why of the product. What are we looking to achieve with this product and why? Which customer problems are we looking to solve and why? What does product success look like and why?

Especially when working with stakeholders, developers, and designers, it is of vital importance that everybody is on the same page with regard to the what and why of the product. It can quickly become counterproductive if people working on or selling the product have not fully bought into what we are looking to achieve and the underlying rationale.

The product manager is ultimately accountable for the what and why of a product. On a daily basis, this translates into communicating continuously with stakeholders, developers, designers, customers, marketing people, suppliers, and so on. You own the overarching product vision and direction of the product, and it is your responsibility to make sure that everyone understands and has bought into the product vision and can take others on a product journey.

In addition, because the what and why are likely to evolve over time, product managers act as the safeguard of this evolution. For instance, when I joined a music streaming service several years ago, the product focus was very much on making music available for digital downloads. As technology and customer needs evolved into music streaming, this meant that our product changed drastically. As a product manager, I played an important part in being on the front foot of that evolution.

How

Returning to Stacy, who I introduced at the beginning of this chapter, I disagree with her in that I believe product managers *should* become be involved in the day-to-day and the how of designing and building products. Building and managing products is a team sport, which implies that product managers have a clear role to play in the execution of product ideas and features.

For example, I have had many fruitful discussions with UX designers on what specific user interfaces should look like and why. Similarly, I love playing devil's advocate to developers, asking why we desperately need certain functionality.[131] This level of involvement excludes the product manager acting as a UX designer or stepping on developers' toes. Ultimately, a UX designer is best placed to make UX designs, and developers will have the technical expertise necessary to decide on how to best achieve the agreed results. It means becoming an integral part of the product team that is accountable for building great products.

Combining the what and why with the how demands that product managers balance the forward-looking tasks of their roles—for example, following the product, creating and adhering to a product strategy, and planning for the next customer or product theme[132]—with key day-to-day responsibilities, which I will further elaborate on in this chapter.

---

[131] "My Product Management Toolkit (9): Playing Devil's Advocate," Marc Abraham, May 7, 2016, https://marcabraham.com/2016/05/07/my-product-management-toolkit-9-playing-devils-advocate/.
[132] "No More Features on Product Roadmaps—Have Themes or Goals Instead!," Marc Abraham, October 1, 2015, https://marcabraham.com/2015/10/01/no-more-features-on-product-roadmaps-have-themes-or-goals-instead/.

Figure 5.1. The product manager is accountable for the what and the why, and the entire product development team is accountable for the how.

2. Common Responsibilities of Day-to-Day Product Management

Now that we have established that, on a daily basis, product managers mix the what and the why with the how and collaborate closely with others in the process, let's take a look at the common responsibilities involved (see also fig. 5.2):

- **Prioritise what to work on.** Deciding what to work on and when is a core responsibility of every product manager. In the next section, we will look at different methods you can use when having to make tough prioritisation decisions.
- **Make trade-off decisions.** Closely linked to prioritisation is the ability to decide on what can be tough trade-offs. For example, do we build feature A or B? Do we add this complexity now or later? How will the overall user experience be affected if we add this feature? These are some of the trade-offs that product managers are presented with on a daily basis.
- **Create and manage a backlog.** Once you have prioritised, you are most likely to have a backlog of prioritised features and tasks. You will be responsible for constantly (re)ordering and communicating this backlog.

- **Know when to terminate a product or feature.** Although this may not be a daily task for most of us, deciding to terminate a feature or product is closely linked to prioritising and deciding on trade-offs.
- **Write user stories, acceptance scenarios, and criteria.** There are several ways in which you could specify what needs to get built and why. User stories and acceptance criteria are an accepted way of capturing requirements in a more user-centric and outcome-oriented way.
- **Determine success, measure feedback, and iterate.** How do we know that a feature is successful? As a product manager, you can set the core metric to be measured and make sure that this metric is being reflected and iterated upon continuously.
- **Say no.** In line with setting priorities and making trade-off decisions, you will end up saying no to a lot of things. Later in this chapter, we will look at different ways in which you can say no.

Naturally, this is not an exhaustive list, and you might not even be doing any of these things on a daily basis. However, these are some core activities that underpin what we do as product managers. I will delve into some of these tasks and provide you with more context and tips about them.

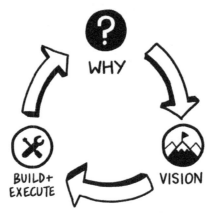

Figure 5.2. Product ideation and development both form part of the same continuous loop.

3. Prioritisation

There are numerous ways you can prioritise the work that needs to be done to build or iterate a product. In this section, I will look at several useful prioritisation methods, but prioritisation ultimately comes down to asking why. In chapter 2, we looked at the importance of continuously asking why, and the same rigour applies to prioritisation:

- *Why* is this piece of work important?
- *Why* should we do this piece of work over another piece of work?
- *Why* now?
- *Why* will customers value us doing this piece of work?
- *Why* should we be doing this work?

There are several prioritisation methods to choose from, and I have selected three that I have found to be helpful and simple to apply.

MoSCoW

The MoSCoW prioritisation method is a straightforward way of prioritising customer and business benefits. Typically, the must-have requirements are prioritised first:[133]

- **Must have:** Requirements labelled as *must have* are critical to the customer and/or business in order for the product to be a success and for the users to receive the product benefits.
- **Should have:** Requirements labelled as *should have* are important but not as critical for the customer and the business as compared to must-have requirements.
- **Could have:** Requirements labelled as *could have* are desirable but not necessary and could improve user experience or customer satisfaction for little development cost.
- **Won't have (this time):** Requirements labelled as *won't have* are those requirements that we agree won't be included (now).

Value versus Risk

When considering the benefits of a particular product or feature, it is just as important to consider risk when prioritising. The nature of the risk to consider can be very diverse—technical, complexity, regulation, timing, and so on. Mapping value against risk helps to identify and prioritise high-value, high-risk items. (See fig. 5.3.)

---

[133] "MoSCoW Method," Wikipedia, last edited February 2, 2018, https://en.wikipedia.org/wiki/MoSCoW_method.

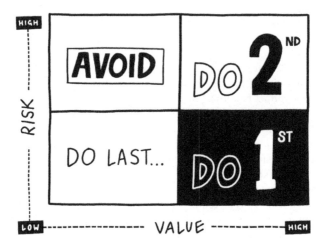

Figure 5.3. Making prioritisation decisions based on perceived value and risk

Story Mapping

Story mapping is probably my favourite prioritisation technique because I have found it to be very effective with respect to facilitating valuable conversations about what we are looking to build, why, and when. Jeff Patton, a well-known user-experience specialist, introduced story maps.[134] Patton's focus is on telling stories instead of concentrating solely on what should be written.

---

[134] Jeff Patton, *User Story Mapping: Discover the Whole Story, Build the Right Product* (Sebastopol, CA: O'Reilly Media, 2014).

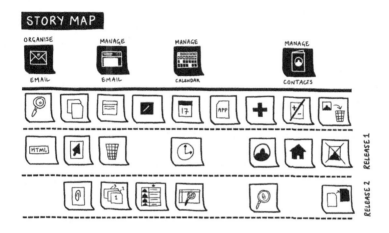

Figure 5.4. Example of a user story map

The following tips will help you to create a story map:

- **Frame your idea first.** The ability to put structure around your product idea is one of the most important benefits of Patton's story-mapping technique. Start with agreeing on desired outcomes for a specific group of customers and users. Once you've gone through the exercise of figuring out what to build, for whom, and why, it should be much easier to prioritise implementation work.
- **Consider breadth over depth.** Patton recommends focussing on the breadth of a story first before delving into the depth of it. This means starting with mapping big activities first and then breaking these down into smaller, more detailed user stories. (See fig. 5.4.) After covering breadth, you can then start exploring details and options per individual user story: What are the specific things my target user would do here? What are alternative things he or she could do? What would make it really cool? What about when things go wrong?

- **Understand that the backbone organises the story map.** With a story map, one typically starts with a backbone, which is formed at the top of the map. This is usually a basic and high-level flow of the story.
- **Expose risk in the story map.** Similar to the value versus risk method, you can use the story map to identify and mitigate risk early in the product development process. Putting a Post-it note with the word *risk* against a user story is a highly effective way of making risk visible and getting people to think about how to best mitigate this risk.

It is fair to say that prioritisation is an ongoing responsibility for most product managers; it happens both at set times and ad hoc. For example, if you work in two-week sprints, you will prioritise every fortnight based on a product backlog. You will be responsible for constantly (re)ordering and communicating this backlog.

4. Saying No

> *The essence of strategy is choosing what not to do.*
> —Michael Porter

Saying no is possibly one of the most challenging parts of being a product manager. There are so many great business and product ideas out there, and ideally, we'd like to do all of them. However, I refer to one of the greatest product people, Steve Jobs, and his views on the importance of saying no: "Focusing is about saying NO."

These are the main reasons why I believe in the importance of saying no:

- **Focus:** We can't do it all. What's truly important and why? Will it move the needle? If so, how?
- **Constraints:** Every business has constraints—people, time, money, opportunities. As a result, saying no sometimes acts as an absolute necessity.
- **Cost and risks:** We need to say no from time to time to manage (opportunity) cost and risks.

As a consequence, every product person benefits from having a few ways of saying no in his or her toolkit. I'll highlight five different options for when you want to say no.

Open the Kimono

Opening the kimono is a popular phrase, but it is effectively just stressing the importance of being fully transparent with others. As a product manager, you are typically in a position to provide full transparency on the following:

- **Vision:** What is our product vision and why? What does success look like?
- **Strategy:** Which steps will we take to achieve our product vision?
- **Road map:** What are the product goals and milestones we are looking to realise over the short to long term?
- **Backlog:** How have specific items been prioritised and why? Where do they sit within the product backlog?
- **Trade-offs:** What are the trade-offs we made whilst prioritising? What was the underlying rationale for these trade-off decisions?
- **Cost:** How much does it cost to build a certain product or feature? Once built, how do actual costs compare to original cost projections? It is also worth being transparent about cost of delay—that is, the cost of not doing a certain piece of work.[135]
- **Value:** How much value will this product bring to the customer? What does the expected business value look like? How do we know that this product is delivering value? Be transparent about value and standard metrics, such as return on investment and gross profit.

---

[135] Donald G. Reinertsen, *The Principles of Product Development Flow: Second Generation Lean Product Development* (Redondo Beach, CA: Celeritas, 2009).

Figure 5.5. Be as transparent as possible.

Opening the kimono—that is, being fully transparent—helps you start a conversation about the potential results of certain decisions. (See fig. 5.5.) Looking back, I feel I've learned most from difficult conversations with internal stakeholders or sponsors that would typically go like this:

> **Sponsor:** Can you please add features A, B, and C to the road map for this quarter?
>
> **Me:** Why?
>
> **Sponsor:** Because we have got this great opportunity with one client!
>
> **Me:** Interesting. Please tell me more.
>
> **Sponsor:** Well, it will generate a lot of revenue if we add these features just for this client.
>
> **Me:** No!

In my early days as a product manager, I would be really thrown by these requests and shut down to the point where I would say, "No. That doesn't fit with our road map." Not only would this approach hurt my relationship with the stakeholder in question but also the stakeholder would often go over my head to get the features prioritised anyway.

Based on my lessons learned, if this type of conversation sounds familiar, I recommend approaching it a bit more like this:

Sponsor: Can you please add features A, B, and C to the road map for this quarter?

You: Why?

Sponsor: Because we have got this great opportunity with one client!

You: Interesting. Please tell me more.

Sponsor: Well, it will generate a lot of revenue if we add these features just for this client.

You: I can see the short-term results, particularly from a revenue point of view. However, I'm worried about the long-term results of adding these highly bespoke features for just this one client.

Sponsor: Why are you worried about the long-term results?

You: Because, from my experience, if you add the cost of supporting and maintaining these features for one client, the cost of undoing technical debt during the entire life cycle of these features, these costs are likely to seriously exceed the immediate revenues. Also, I'm worried about the cost of delay when we add these features instead of the items originally prioritised for this quarter. I believe that the opportunity cost of not entering markets X, Y, and Z will be high, as our competitors are likely to get ahead of us in these markets."

Sponsor: OK. That makes sense. Can you please give me some estimates for the costs you are talking about?"

You: Of course. I'll compare and contrast these costs against the revenues of your opportunity to help us make an informed decision.

I have had some good successes with this approach because it has allowed me to have a data-informed conversation with stakeholders, encouraging them to look at the bigger picture. Instead of a blunt no, providing a simple but objective cost-benefit analysis has led to sponsors deciding to prefer long-term value over short-term gains.

Scope Small and Test Assumptions

A few years ago, design practitioner Peter Merholz, then at Adaptive Path, introduced a cake analogy that I absolutely love.[136] Merholz visualises two ways to bake a wedding cake. (See fig. 5.6.) One way is to create a big wedding cake, starting with a cake base and adding the filling and icing. Alternatively, you can start with a small cupcake and see what the soon-to-be-married couple thinks about it, after which you can decide to make another cupcake or a proper wedding cake. The key here is that you're not saying no and shutting the door on an idea or project. In contrast, you're proposing to start small and to get real user feedback often and early:

- **Scope small:** "I suggest we don't commit to the entire product or project up-front. Instead, I suggest we focus on a single feature or value component first and measure its effect. We can then always decide to do more and iterate."
- **Test assumptions:** "We assume that our users need tomato juice to quench their thirst. How can we best validate this quickly before we commit to making tomato juice?"

---

[136] "Cupcakes: The Secret to Product Planning," Brandon Schauer, Adaptive Path, February 10, 2011, http://adaptivepath.org/ideas/cupcakes-the-secret-to-product-planning/; "Start with a Cupcake," Des Traynor, Intercom, accessed February 3, 2018, https://blog.intercom.com/start-with-a-cupcake/.

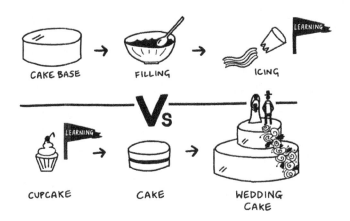

Figure 5.6. Peter Merholz's two ways of baking a wedding cake[137]

Consider Side Effects

If you use time-to-build to prioritize what to build next, you'll end up with a product full of easy solutions.

—Teresa Torres[138]

We all know how easy it can be to say yes to an idea or an improvement that sounds small or quick to build. However, in doing so, we often forget that even the smallest of features or changes can have a big result. There are several potential side effects to consider before saying yes or no:

- **Development cost:** What are the costs of creating this? What does the expected return on investment look like and why?

---

[137] Image based on: "Start with a Cupcake," Des Traynor, Intercom, accessed February 3, 2018, https://blog.intercom.com/start-with-a-cupcake/.
[138] "The Simplest (and Most Important) Question You Face as a Product Leader," Teresa Torres, Product Talk, February 27, 2014, https://www.producttalk.org/2014/02/the-simplest-and-most-important-question-you-face-as-a-product-leader/.

- **Maintenance cost:** Can we maintain it? What are the costs involved in doing so?
- **Support cost:** What is required to support the product and its users? What are the ongoing support costs?
- **Business model:** How does this fit with our business model and its commercial targets?
- **System influence:** Are there any ramifications on the wider system or technical/organisational infrastructure?
- **Technical debt:** Will we incur technical debt as a result of this feature or change?
- **Unhappy customers:** By doing this, will we alienate clients?

Not Now

There will be plenty of situations where you will decide to do something later instead of right away. It is therefore not a straight no but something we could do at a later stage. For example, "Let's do this once we've implemented our new shopping cart feature, as it will be easier to add this feature on then. We will add this to the 'next' section on our road map."

One word of warning: I've seen many people use this approach to kick things into the long grass, burying things into the road map or backlog in the hope that it is forgotten. This is counterproductive and dishonest. If you already know that something isn't going to get done, then it's better to be transparent about this up-front. (See fig. 5.7.)

Figure 5.7. No can be the answer to product or feature requests.

Provide Options

Instead of offering a downright no, provide options and explore the pros and cons of each option. I've found that this approach really helps in having a constructive conversation with business stakeholders about business goals and trade-offs. Consider the following options:

Option 1: Build on top of existing APIs.
- Pros: speed to market, less costly, meet partner expectations
- Cons: not scalable, opportunity cost

Option 2: Create the API framework first and then create new API endpoints.
- Pros: fully scalable, revenue and partnership opportunities
- Cons: takes longer to develop and will be more costly

Saying no and declining a feature request or an idea can be hard but also very necessary. Although it can feel a tad uncomfortable, there's a lot of value in saying no in a more informed and constructive kind of way.

5. Knowing When and How to Retire a Product or Feature

Kill a feature every week. When you kill the wrong one, people will make noise and you'll be clued into what actually adds value.
—Dave McClure, founding partner of 500 Startups[139]

Thus far we have looked only at building new products and adding features. However, deciding to terminate a product or feature is also a product manager's responsibility. Not only is simply continuing to add features to a product likely to kill it fast but also discontinuing products or features will help to keep the integrity of the product's value proposition fully intact.

In this section, we will look at when and why to discontinue a product or feature. I will also provide some pointers on how to best terminate a product or feature.

When and Why

There are several signs and circumstances that indicate your product or feature is ready to be terminated:

- **Customers don't want it anymore.** Whether customers are still interested in your product will typically become apparent very quickly. Usage data and real user feedback are likely to leave little doubt as soon as a product starts to fizzle out. In the next paragraph, we will look more at usage data and more generally using data to inform product decisions.
- **Customers are confused by your product.** Many times, I have seen customers become confused by the number of bells and whistles on a product and thus lose focus on the core problem the product was looking to

---

[139] "Startup Metrics for Pirates & KILL A FEATURE!" Dave McClure, October 2, 2009, http://500hats.typepad.com/500blogs/2009/10/startup-metrics-for-pirates-kill-a-feature-fowa-london-oct-2009.html.

solve. I call this featuritis.[140] As a result, customers don't know what to make of a product or how to use it.
- **The product doesn't generate revenue and margin.** The financial numbers for your product stop adding up, such as when revenue growth stagnates or when the gross profit margin per product starts declining rapidly. Cost can be another indicator of the necessity to kill a product; think of the cost to support a product, for example.
- **The company has moved on to other products.** Lisa Long, vice president of product management at Telenor, frequently talks about zombie features.[141] These features are often historic ones and are usually unused and unloved. Typically, you can easily spot these features when the company has moved on to new and shinier ones, and the look feels very different from those that have been left behind, so to speak. It often is reflected in a customer experience that feels very convoluted, made up of old and new bits.
- **No one internally is clear about why the product or feature exists.** Another symptom associated with zombie features is that nobody currently working in the company knows why the feature exists or how it works under the hood. "This was built before my time, and I'd rather not touch it" is a comment I have heard often.

How

Once you have detected one or more of the previous signs, it is worth considering terminating your product or feature. Just as you need to carefully plan a product launch, it is just as important to think through how to best retire a product. For example, people who have been using the product until the point of discontinuation suddenly can't use the product anymore and enjoy the benefits of it. This raises the question of how to best terminate a product or feature gracefully.

Craig Strong, a technology and product leader at Hubble, has identified ten useful points to consider when retiring your product.[142] Strong's ten points make for a good checklist to go through once you have decided to terminate your product or feature.

[140] "My Product Management Toolkit (10): Jobs-to-Be-Done," Marc Abraham, June 2, 2016, https://marcabraham.com/2016/06/02/my-product-management-toolkit-10-jobs-to-be-done/.
[141] "How to Survive the Product Zombie Apocalypse," Chris Massey, Mind the Product, October 31, 2016, https://www.mindtheproduct.com/2016/10/survive-product-zombie-apocalypse/.
[142] "How and Why You Should Retire Products in Your Portfolio," Craig Strong, Strong and Agile Digital Product Development, January 29, 2017, http://www.strongandagile.co.uk/index.php/how-and-why-you-should-retire-products-in-your-portfolio/.

1. **Have you identified and met the service-level agreements (SLAs) considering third-party commitments?** You might have decided to retire a product because it's not providing the return you need, but your product might belong to an ecosystem with contractual SLAs in place. Failing to observe and explore these SLAs could result in legal repercussions that could far exceed the cost of keeping the product active and alive. Look to identify these first before making any decisions, and consider the effect on your brand and other strategic opportunities against the impact of product retirement.

2. **Do you have sufficient customer service in place to manage the additional customer support required to handle the retirement phase?** When you decide to retire your product, you should expect to increase investment in customer service and support for a specific duration. Following a retirement announcement, existing customers will understandably have many concerns, and this will likely spike a demand for customer service and support. Knowing this will help inform a communications plan with your marketing team to manage the messaging and support of retirement. You will also need to train and align the support teams.

3. **Do you have sufficient technical capabilities to manage the strategic retirement phase?** Just as you need to invest in customer service, diligence should be undertaken on existing skills needed and available to manage the retirement of your product. On retiring a product, you may need to employ or source new skills specialised in some of the tasks needed at retirement. Consider, for instance, data management. You will likely need to manage the destruction of customer data securely and destroy or reconstitute hardware if it's to be repurposed.

4. **Have you identified dependencies and communicated to all business areas how this affects them, and provided a coordinated plan?** This is particularly important for larger enterprises. Investigating the effect on dependent systems is an exercise well worth undertaking. It never ceases to surprise me how small systems sitting in the corner somewhere are unknowingly providing valuable contributions to the better-known products elsewhere in the organisation. This exercise not only increases the value of the system being marked for retirement but also reduces risk by calling out the impact required to manage any transitions or upgrades needed.

5. **Do you have sufficient marketing, communications strategies, and resources to support the retirement phase?** Resources will be required to systematically inform internal users, third parties, and customers of a

retirement decision. This will require strategic communications with managed timelines and review points and focussed marketing to handle the retirement. This may also include upselling an alternative product as well as offering users options to migrate their data to different systems.

6. **Have you identified how assets and resources can be utilised and offered to other parts of the business or other products?** Consider the retirement of products as a learning opportunity. Before closing the door on a product, consider what could be learned and retained. You are likely to have experienced staff who could add considerable value elsewhere in the business. You might also have in-depth knowledge of the product use data that other products could use, processes that could be shared, and much more. Don't overlook the potential value that can be shared for the benefit to the rest of the existing organisation. You should look to retain your human talent above all; if this is not carefully managed, it will result in a potential brain drain.

7. **Have you protected and provided options for customers to export their data?** It is good practice and, in some cases, mandatory to consider developing solutions so that customers who use your product can move their data elsewhere or download it for future use. This will prevent customer angst and will also help you retain customers if moving them to other products. With so many products available, even products that are not being marked for retirement allow for the easy transport of customer-owned data so that customers can integrate it into other platforms.

8. **Has the pipeline of acquiring new customer acquisitions been closed and strategically managed?** When a product is selected for retirement, it's important to close the pipeline of new customer acquisitions. This may include the capability of signing up for the product or creating an account on a digital platform. You should extend this to discovering the product through various channels and informing sales and marketing so that no future sales will be negotiated.

9. **Have all finances been identified and resolved?** In accordance with the previous questions, all retirement costs should be identified and proposed. It's expected when executing the retirement of a product that additional finances will be required to manage the previous points. In addition to this, any products costs and revenue should be resolved for financial forecasts.

10. **Have alternative products been identified to transition customers?** Customers should be offered product alternatives whenever possible. Transition opportunities should be identified, and migration expectations should inform the retirement strategy. Customer migration paths and processes to make this as painless as possible for customers are key to

protect revenue, not only for the product but also for the larger company brand.

The music service This Is My Jam is a good example of a product that was retired well.[143] This Is My Jam let users collect and stream their favourite songs, but it had to shut down, mostly due to scalability issues.[144] Instead of an abrupt service shutdown, This Is My Jam users can, to this day, still access their tracks and personal descriptions in a read-only mode and listen to them via the site or as Spotify playlists. In addition, there was a time window in which users could export their tracks, likes, and more information as they wished.

Going back to the when and why part of this section, This Is My Jam is a good example of a company that saw the writing on the wall early and then moved on to determine how to best deprecate its product and associated features.

6. Using Data to Inform Product Decisions

It is a capital mistake to theorise before one has data.
—Sir Arthur Conan Doyle

In the previous section, we saw that usage data can be a clear indicator of people no longer being interested in a product. Quantitative data especially can reflect how a product has petered out. As product managers, data should be one of our best friends, if not the best. We will therefore look at the following data-related aspects in this section:

- Why do we need data?
- What can quantitative data tell us?
- What can qualitative data tell us?
- What is the difference between data driven and data informed?
- What is the contextual nature of usage data?
- When and why do we use data?

You might recall the hypothesis statement we looked at in the previous chapter or even when we looked at value and viability—data is paramount. My simple adage

---

[143] "Why I Really Like This Is My Jam," Marc Abraham, July 12, 2012, https://marcabraham.com/2012/07/12/why-i-really-like-this-is-my-jam/; "Despite Impending Shutdown, 'This Is My Jam' to Preserve User Data," Nathaniel Mott, Gigaom, August 10, 2015, https://gigaom.com/2015/08/10/despite-impending-shutdown-this-is-my-jam-to-preserve-user-data/.
[144] "This Is My Jam Shuts Down without Screwing Users," Josh Constine, TechCrunch, August 9, 2015, https://techcrunch.com/2015/08/09/dont-make-us-fear-the-reaper/.

is that some data are better than no data. Whether you are deciding to create a new product or to end it, data will help you to make a decision.

Whether you are looking at ways to gather, collate, or analyse data, they are likely to be an important part of your day-to-day responsibilities as a product manager. Data are an important means to an end—product decisions being the end in the case of product management.

Why Do We Need Data?

I am always keen to stress that as a product manager, I do not have all the answers. Product managers are not the holy grail, and it would be silly and disingenuous to pretend otherwise. Even when people look to me for answers or assurance, I am not afraid to say that I am not fully certain whether our product idea will be a guaranteed hit or how people will use our product and that I will need to study the data to provide a better answer.[145] This does not mean that I am a fan of analysis paralysis, endlessly mulling over data (and delaying your decision).

At some point you will have to take a leap of faith, especially with completely new products, as long as you then start measuring *actual* product performance and customer behaviours. Up until that point, everything is just assumptions, mere speculation.

What Can Quantitative Data Tell Us?

Quantitative data can help generate the statistics on how people *actually* use a product and measure whether our product improvements or new features have the desired result. For example, if I wish to learn how many people have downloaded my app in the past month, I can quickly view download stats from the app store data. Similarly, using common analytics packages, such as Google Analytics or Mixpanel, can give you a better understanding of the average conversion rate of your customers.

What Can Qualitative Data Tell Us?

Qualitative data can be very valuable if you want to discover the why behind quantitative data and to gain better insight into what users think and feel. For

---

[145] "Using Data to Inform Product Decisions," Marc Abraham, August 18, 2014, https://marcabraham.com/2014/08/18/using-data-to-inform-product-decisions/.

example, if you are disappointed with the sudden dip in download figures for your app, the app store data are unlikely to give you many helpful insights. However, by talking to target customers, you are much more likely to learn about what is wrong and why people have not been downloading it.

Also, in cases when you do not have much quantitative data at your disposal to be begin with, qualitative data can help you to get some quick input into a product idea or prototype. This is most likely to be the case if you work at an early-stage start-up or when you are creating a new product.

What is the Difference between Data Driven and Data Informed?

Several game companies, such as Zynga and Wooga, apply a strictly data-driven approach to product development. This typically means that a company will pick a single key metric or a set to concentrate on. For instance, Wooga focusses on a single retention metric during a certain period. In that period, all its efforts will be focussed on optimising the chosen retention metric. A multitude of A/B experiments are carried out to establish which design or functionality moves the needle on the single metric. If any of these experiments show a clear winner in terms of design or functionality, they will concentrate most of their efforts on optimising this design or functionality. Thus, with a purely data-driven approach, it's data that determine the faith of a product. Based on data outcomes, businesses can optimise continuously for the biggest result on their key metric.

In contrast, with a data-informed approach, data are only one factor to consider when making product decisions and developing products. The main rationale for this data-informed approach is that, in reality, data are only one of the factors to consider when making product decisions.

I learned a lot from Adam Mosseri, vice president of product management at Facebook, in this respect.[146] Before coming across Mosseri's talk, I thought that Facebook would be 100 percent data driven given that it sits on an abundance of user data. However, Mosseri explained how Facebook looks at several factors when making a product decision, such as strategy, regulation, intuition, user experience, and technology. This data-informed approach doesn't diminish the critical nature of data, but it does take into account a reality where other factors must be considered when making product decisions.

---

[146] "Data Informed, Not Data Driven," Adam Mosseri, accessed February 3, 2018, https://vimeo.com/14999991.

What Is the Contextual Nature of Usage Data?

Looking at only one piece of data in isolation often tells just a (small) part of the story. For example, should an average conversion rate of 3 percent be considered high or low? This all depends on the context of the usage metric in question. These are some of the contextual questions you should ask of the data:

- **Does the product have a time-bound or seasonal nature?** A product can be highly seasonal and therefore mostly used during a certain period of the year. For instance, when I worked at an e-commerce marketplace, all metrics used to shoot through the roof in December when people visited the site to buy Christmas gifts.
- **What customer needs does the product solve, and what are typical customer behaviours?** Certain products enjoy a limited use due to the nature and frequency of consumer needs and behaviours. For example, there are several financial products—for example, wealth management and pensions—that people will use infrequently, but when to do it can have a big influence. These usage patterns should be taken into account when looking at data.
- **Is there an internal or external benchmark figure?** In certain industries, there are benchmark data you can use as a rule of thumb to put the performance of your product in context. This might sound high when referring to the 3 percent conversion rate mentioned earlier, but it takes on a different significance if the industry standard is a 5 percent conversion rate. In the same vein, 3 percent might be considered good performance if the same rate historically used to be around the 1 percent mark.

Where and Why to Use Data to Help Inform Product Decisions

There are several cases when a purely data-driven approach falls short. For example, when there's a strategic decision to be made or when you're assessing a new product idea, looking at data in isolation may be insufficient. Here are some examples of how and why I use data at set points of the product life cycle to help inform decision making:

- **What do we want to do and why?** Assumptions, hypotheses, assessments, and prototypes
- **How should it work?** User testing, user stories, A/B testing, and prototypes
- **How is it working?** Performance tracking, comparing, and goal-oriented planning

In conclusion, data are likely to play a big part in your day-to-day responsibilities as a product manager. Even if you don't work in a data-driven environment, it is important to analyse and use data to at least *inform* your product decisions.

7. Writing User Stories and Acceptance Scenarios or Acceptance Criteria

The goal of using stories isn't to write better stories. The goal of product development is to make products.

—Jeff Patton

In the previous chapter, we talked about the importance of storytelling for product managers. Telling a compelling product story will help you to share the customer problems to solve and the results the product is aiming to have for the customer group in question. The next steps are user stories and acceptance criteria.

User Stories

Writing user stories means you are translating the bigger stories in specific user outcomes to design and build. User stories are short descriptions of functionality to build, explaining a change in user behaviour to achieve. In this section, we will look at writing user stories and acceptance criteria in more detail.

The canonical format for user stories is written as follows:[147]

As a _____, I want _____ so that _____.

As a [type of user], I want [to achieve a specific goal] so that [reason why, perceived benefit].

Now that we know the common components of a user story, let's look at two simple examples:

As an ice cream vendor,
I want to use my phone to keep track of the number of ice cream tubs sold
So that I can do my bookkeeping on the go.

---

[147] "User Stories," Mike Cohn, Mountain Goat Software, accessed February 3, 2018, https://www.mountaingoatsoftware.com/agile/user-stories.

As a hairdresser,
I want to show customers examples of the hairstyles I have cut
So that customers can tell me exactly how they would like their hair to be cut.

As you can see from these simple examples, user stories don't have to be complex or lengthy. I have seen people write novel-style user stories. Unfortunately, lengthy and complicated user stories tend to be impractical when it comes to other reading and implementing.

User stories need to be clear and concise and spell out the specific user outcome the feature is trying to achieve. As a useful rule of thumb, I tend to use Bill Wake's INVEST model when writing user stories.[148] Wake is a Lean and Agile software development consultant, and his INVEST model offers a nice way to summarise user stories:

- Independent: The user story should be self-contained in a way that there is no inherent dependency on another user story.
- Negotiable: Up until they are part of an iteration, user stories can always be changed and rewritten.
- Valuable: A user story must deliver value to the end user.
- Estimable: You must always be able to estimate the size of a user story.
- Small: User stories should not be so big as to become impossible to plan/task/prioritise with a given level of certainty.
- Testable: The user story or its related description must provide the necessary information to make test development possible.

One of my biggest bugbears with respect to writing user stories is that they should be the result of a solo effort by the product manager or product owner. Wrong. Effective, actionable user stories are the result of a collaborative effort, with key people involved in executing the user stories reviewing and adding to the user stories they will be implementing.

The classic mistake is for a product manager to write a user story and then throw it over an imaginary wall to the designers or developers who have to implement it. The user story is an artefact, and I strongly believe that the conversation about a user story is just as critical as writing it in the first place. Ron Jeffries, a well-

---

[148] "INVEST in Good Stories, and SMART Tasks," Bill Wake, EXP123, August 17, 2003, https://xp123.com/articles/invest-in-good-stories-and-smart-tasks/.

known Agile software development consultant, identifies three phases associated with the user story artefact: card, conversation, and confirmation:[149]

- A *card* (or often a Post-it note) is a physical token that gives tangible and durable form to what would otherwise be only an abstraction.
- A *conversation* at different times and places during a project among the various people concerned about a given feature of a software product: customers, users, developers, testers; this conversation is largely verbal but is most often supplemented by documentation.
- The *confirmation*—the more formal the better—is when the objectives the conversation revolved around have been reached.

Acceptance Scenarios

User stories help to capture specific outcomes that you want the product to achieve for its users. A user story is then accompanied by acceptance criteria, which are usually presented as scenarios. These scenarios are meant to help establish when a feature is done or complete.

The key elements of a scenario are the title (one line describing the scenario), given (context), and (some more context), and then (outcome). For example:

> **Title:** Number of ice cream tubs is running low
> **Given** that I have turned on my ice cream alert
> **And** there are fewer than five tubs of ice cream left in my freezer
> **When** I open the door of my freezer
> **Then** I receive an alert on my phone letting me know that I am running out of ice cream, and I can order it and fill up my freezer

Normally I find it easiest to start by describing a so-called happy path, a scenario whereby the desired outcome is achieved, and everything goes according to plan. From this ideal scenario, you can then derive several edge cases, scenarios that throw a spanner in the works of the happy path. For example:

> **Title:** Number of ice cream tubs is running low
> **Given** that I have turned on my ice cream alert
> **And** the monitoring sensor in my freezer is not working

---

[149] "Essential XP: Card, Conversation, Confirmation," Ron Jeffries, August 30, 2001, https://ronjeffries.com/xprog/articles/expcardconversationconfirmation/.

And there are fewer than five tubs of ice cream left in my freezer
When I open the door of my freezer
Then I will receive an error notification via my phone letting me know that I need to replace my freezer sensor and that I need to check my ice cream stock manually.

Acceptance Criteria

Whether you have determined a happy path or an edge case, you can now start identifying the individual acceptance criteria that your product needs to meet to satisfy the customer and that will need to be implemented.[150] Acceptance criteria are a set of statements made up of specific functional and nonfunctional requirements that must be met.
The main benefit of acceptance scenarios is that they are testable. You can recreate these test conditions and make sure that your product meets the agreed acceptance criteria. For example:

- The ice cream app needs to work on both iOS and Android.
- A warning notification needs to be sent to the user when there are five or fewer ice cream tubs left in the freezer.
- The copy of the warning notification needs to read: "Your stock is running low! Please order or make more ice cream tubs!"

In conclusion, an important benefit of user stories, acceptance scenarios, and criteria is that they offer a common language through which people can communicate what it is they are trying to achieve and the scope of the work involved. Another key benefit is that stories and scenarios are testable, whether testing is done in an automated or nonautomated fashion.

8. Three Questions and Answers: How to Deal with Daily Product Management Challenges

A great product manager has the brain of an engineer, the heart of a designer, and the speech of a diplomat.
—Deep Nishar, managing partner at SoftBank Vision Fund

So far in this chapter, we have looked at the various aspects and tools of daily product management. Let's put some of these to the test and apply them to some common challenges you are likely to face on a regular basis as a product manager.

Question 1: You need to plan for a next iteration of work. How do you this?

Answer 1: Ask yourself what, why, and why now.

You might want to start by looking at your product road map, if you have one, to determine the priorities for the upcoming iteration or sprint. The road map should outline the overarching product direction for the coming weeks or months. Whether you have a road map or not, it's important to ask yourself the following questions for each individual item of work:

What is this piece of work?

- A new feature
- Implementing a new service
- Fixing a bug
- Improving an existing feature

Why is this piece of work important?

- Because it addresses a user need or problem
- Because it solves an important bug or issue with the current product or experience
- Because this item is a prerequisite for another piece of work
- Because another team is dependent on this work getting done
- Because it is required for a revenue-generating business opportunity

Why will customers value us doing this piece of work?

- It will solve a critical problem they have.
- It will have a tangible influence on their life.
- It will help them save time doing a specific task.
- It will help them save money doing a specific task.

Why should we do this piece of work over another piece of work?

- Because we expect the result for the customer to be higher

- Because we expect the result for business success or performance to be greater
- Because this item is a prerequisite for another piece of work
- Because another team is dependent on this work getting done
- Because this piece of work is an absolute must have

Why now?

- There are deadlines in place that cannot be moved (such as being set by a regulator or supplier).
- If we do not solve the problem now, the business will (continue to) lose money.
- We feel that we have a competitive advantage if we do it now.
- We have a great business opportunity that is time sensitive.
- The cost of delay is high. In other words, the cost of not doing this piece of work now is significant.
- There is a seasonal element to this work, which means that it is important to do it now.

Question 2: A new product idea or request has come in, with the expectation that it be done now. How do you handle this?

Answer 2: Consider whether it's worth doing now or prioritising later.

The challenge of a stakeholder requesting a feature to be done now or a bug to solve now is likely a common one for those of you reading this. Even if your first instinct is to say no, there are a few things to consider and communicate to the stakeholder in question: Is it worth doing now, later, or not at all?

Use the MoSCoW prioritisation technique to establish whether this requested item is a must have, should have, could have, or won't have. Especially when you are thinking of deprioritising existing work, I recommend weighing the value and risks associated with the new piece of work and contrasting these aspects with the work prioritised or in flight. If the value and risk of the new piece of work are high, there is an argument to do this work first.

Question 3: What do we need to design or build and why?

Answer 3: Use story maps, problem statements, and acceptance scenarios to tell a story.

When it is up to you as a product manager to provide direction to others on what you are looking to design or build and why, there are three techniques you will find helpful:

1. **Customer problem statements:** Start by telling a story about the customer problem(s) you are looking to tackle and explain the effect of these problems on customer lives. Also paint a picture of how we know that we have solved the customer problem.
2. **Story mapping:** Next, you can do a story-map exercise with your team to explain what the customer is looking to achieve and why, working through the different user tasks and product functionality, starting with the most critical tasks.
3. **Acceptance scenarios:** Once you have identified customer tasks, you can break these down into more granular acceptance scenarios. What are the different happy paths and edge cases that the product or feature needs to meet and why?

Key Takeaways

Ultimately, day-to-day product management is about curiosity and collaboration. Good product managers are those who stay curious and are happy to try, learn, and try again. It is a misconception that product managers are lone rock stars. Quite the opposite, you are heavily dependent on others and are therefore expected to provide direction and guidance.

1. **You are accountable for the what and why and jointly responsible for the how.** As a product manager, you are accountable for the what and why of a product. This means that you drive the strategic direction and are responsible for prioritising product features on a daily basis. In contrast, the how of a product is a response shared with designers and developers. Figuring out how the product should work or what it should look like is a shared responsibility.
2. **Prioritise and be able to say no in the face of trade-offs.** Prioritisation is a core product management responsibility. From product inception through to retiring a product, you will be presented with difficult trade-off decisions and prioritisation calls. As hard as it can sometimes be, I encourage you to focus and prioritise ruthlessly, as long you have clear data or grounds on which to base your decision.

3. **Have a plan but start small.** Prototypes and wireframes allow you to test a plan for your product and to learn about its navigation, content, and user flow. This doesn't, however, mean that you need to implement and launch the full functionality set or user flow in one go. An iterative, MVP-driven approach allows you to get customer feedback early and often and to mitigate risk on a continuous basis.

How to Apply These Takeaways

- **Facilitate a story-mapping exercise to get started.** Story mapping is a valuable way to kick off product design and development work. It helps you to provide direction to the rest of your team about what they are trying to achieve with a product, for whom, and why. A collaboratively created story map creates a shared understanding of priority features and interactions.
- **Start with an MVP and measure, learn, and iterate.** An MVP is a useful way to start small when you launch a product whilst still delivering tangible value to the customer. Don't fall into the trap of launching an MVP without iteration unless you have learned that people don't want to buy your product. Measuring is key here, as data will give you the input to feed into subsequent product decisions.
- **Use cost of delay to manage the tensions between short-term gains and long-term benefits.** Often you will be confronted with stakeholders or executive sponsors who favour immediate gains over long-term value. When you face this challenge, outline the different options available—short and long(er) term—and compare and contrast cost of delay in scenarios where the immediate opportunity would prevail versus one where the agreed product direction and road map would be followed.

6
Managing People

Goal

To recognise that product management is a team sport and that soft skills are important to any product person.

Related Tools and Techniques to Consider

- Determine the **typical actors** in day-to-day product management.
- Identify how best to **collaborate** with these actors on a day-to-day basis.
- Start improving your communication skills by **listening actively**.
- **Influence without authority**: techniques to influence.

Introduction

People are definitely a company's greatest asset. It doesn't make any difference whether the product is cars or cosmetics. A company is only as good as the people it keeps.
—Mary Kay Ash, founder of Mary Kay Cosmetics

Let me start this final chapter with a personal confession. In my career thus far, I have made a lot of mistakes or done things that I would now do differently. I guess this applies to most professionals, so there are no surprises there. However, if there is one thing I wish I would have learned sooner, it's stakeholder empathy. I have learned that managing people is a quintessential part of being a product manager.

My confession revolves around the story of when I joined an organisation a few years ago, coming in as its first product person. The organisation had grown rapidly in a short time, without having a product management function. Filled with enthusiasm, I made some mistakes that I have seen other product managers make since:

- **Not listening:** I came in with my set opinions and did not spend enough time observing and listening. Instead of figuring out why my new colleagues were doing things a certain way or trying to truly listen, I made up my mind that my colleagues simply didn't know what they were doing.
- **Being mindless:** With the things I was noticing in my new work environment, I chose to just dismiss them instead of engaging with them.

Ellen Langer, psychology professor at Harvard, refers to this approach as mindlessness.[151] Because I felt I already knew the answer or had the "right" approach, I didn't pay any further attention to some of the organisation's existing ways of working or to the people doing certain tasks. I ruffled quite a few feathers, something that could have been avoided by simply looking at things from a different perspective.

- **Making assumptions:** I still kick myself when I think back to the number of assumptions I made—assumptions about people, processes, customers, and many others. In hindsight, I can now see how much making assumptions was linked to not listening and being mindless. Had I at least checked some of my assumptions, my behaviour would have been somewhat forgivable, but I didn't. As a result, I alienated some great and valuable colleagues almost from day one.
- **Not picking my battles:** Have you ever come across people who are expert at finding something to complain about? That was me. I wanted to improve everything, from the way the organisation engaged with customers to how they referred to developers as resources. Consequently, I acted like a bull in a china shop and upset several people in the process. (See fig. 6.1.)

---

[151] "Mindfulness Isn't Much Harder than Mindlessness," Ellen Langer, *Harvard Business Review*, January 13, 2016, https://hbr.org/2016/01/mindfulness-isnt-much-harder-than-mindlessness.

Figure 6.1. Acting like a bull in a china shop when I joined a business as a product manager

We are all human, so communication or behavioural mistakes are easily made. However, you can possess all the great product management skills in the world, but they are useless if we don't get buy-in from others and collaborate.

In this final chapter, we will look at several specific things that can help you start off on the right foot or provide you with options in a tricky situation: (1) using shared goals, (2) active listening, (3) giving and receiving feedback, and (4) dealing with difficult people. I am not saying these things will act as a silver bullet, but they can prevent you from acting like a bull in a china shop.

1. Typical Collaborators (People to Manage)

Before we delve into specific tools and techniques you can use to manage people, let's first look at the people you're likely to engage with as a product manager. Naturally, the frequency and type of people you will deal with is dependent on the size and type of organisation you work in, but the following stakeholder types and responsibilities tend to be quite common:

- **Sales team:** I'm pretty sure it's the bane of many a product manager's life: a salesperson who's already sold a product that doesn't exist yet or one who has promised a new feature for an existing product. Unfortunately, this is not a feature you have prioritised. This is by no means meant as a slight to salespeople. At the end of the day, they are doing what they are supposed to: selling.[152]
- **Senior management team:** Whether it's the CEO of a corporation or the founder of a start-up, as product managers we often work closely with members of the C-suite or are directly affected by their decisions or plans. For example, a decision by the CEO or management team to enter a new market is likely to have a direct effect on a product.
- **Customers:** If you manage a direct-to-consumer product, you will seek and get feedback directly from your (target) customers. In chapter 3, I mentioned the risk of simply asking customers what they want (and forgetting to ask why). In the case of business-to-business products, you must consider two separate customer groups: the customers who buy your product and their end users who will actually use the product. More often than not, the people buying your product will not be using it on a regular basis.[153]
- **Developers and designers:** Especially for those with an engineering or design background, in your role as a product manager, you're not supposed to write code or create high-fidelity designs. Instead, your responsibility is to provide direction to developers and designers. You are creating the conditions necessary for the team to design and build great products.[154]
- **Compliance:** I could have mentioned numerous internal departments to consider as key internal stakeholders, but I decided to highlight the importance of the internal compliance team. I have often seen the compliance team dubbed internally as the antisales team, people who allegedly wake up in the morning plotting how they can best create more red tape or block new revenue opportunities. Buying into this stereotype is a dangerous pitfall. Instead, it is much more productive to involve your compliance colleagues early and often and to be fully transparent. The risk of not following such an approach is that you end up with a whole lot of stress and headache *after* you've built a product.[155]

---

[152] See "Getting Sales + Product in Sync," Melissa Perri, Medium, April 24, 2017, https://medium.com/pminsider/getting-sales-product-in-sync-aadf14739845.

[153] "End User Customers Matter in B2B," Matt Watson, Hunter Business, September 9, 2017, http://www.hunterbusiness.com/blog/sales-effectiveness/end-user-customers-matter-in-b2b.

[154] See "Let's Talk about Product Management," Josh Elman, October 26, 2015, https://news.greylock.com/let-s-talk-about-product-management-d7bc5606e0c4.

[155] See "5 Product Compliance Best Practices of Leading Companies," Jean-Gregoire Manoukian, Enablon, April 13, 2017, https://enablon.com/blog/2017/04/13/5-product-compliance-best-practices-of-leading-companies.

Effective communication is essential, regardless of the type of stakeholder you come across. In the next section, we will look at ways to engender effective collaboration with stakeholders.

2. How Shared Goals Drive Effective Collaboration

Collaborating constantly can be hard. You may recall from chapter 1 that the role of a product manager is a broad one, with product managers wearing many hats. To act as the connecting factor between customer, business, and technology interests, it is imperative that product managers work closely with other business functions.

One could easily write an entire book about effective collaboration. That is not my intention, as there are already a lot of useful collaboration books out there.[156] Instead, I will concentrate on how shared goals can encourage close collaboration. "To put the first person on the moon" or "to make buying a home as easy as buying bread" are simple examples of shared goals; these are challenges or aspirations that a group of people can rally behind. You don't need to know straightaway how to achieve a certain goal; that is where collaboration comes in—the outcome of effective collaboration is achieving a goal.

As a product manager, there are limitations to the things you can influence. You can, however, influence the creation and prioritisation of goals. In the following case study, I provide an example of how goals can bring people together to create a shared focus. For a goal to be able to generate buy-in, it must be clearly defined and easily understood.[157] It is important for the goal to resonate with many people so that they can see how collaboration contributes to a cause larger than that of any individual:

- What problems are we looking to solve together?
- Why are we tackling these problems?
- How do we know we have solved these problems?
- By when do these problems need to be solved?

[156] See, for example, David Straus, *How to Make Collaboration Work: Powerful Ways to Build Consensus, Solve Problems, and Make Decisions* (San Francisco: Berrett-Koehler, 2002); Robert Keith Sawyer, *Group Genius: The Creative Power of Collaboration* (New York: Basic Books, 2007).
[157] "A Shared Purpose Drives Collaboration," Vineet Nayar, *Harvard Business Review*, April 2, 2014, https://hbr.org/2014/04/a-shared-purpose-drives-collaboration.

For goals to be effective, they need to be defined properly. You've likely come across the term *SMART goals* before. The key thinking behind SMART goals is that they should be easier to understand, measure, and know when they are done.[158] SMART is an acronym that stands for the following:

S = specific, significant, stretching
M = measurable, meaningful, motivational
A = attainable, agreed upon, assignable, acceptable, action oriented
R = realistic, relevant, reasonable, rewarding, results oriented
T = time based, time bound, timely, tangible, measurable

Let me share an example of a SMART goal that I have defined and used previously:

Launching a marketplace for buying and selling homes:

- **Specific:** We will improve the way in which we make it easy for homebuyers and sellers to transact online.
- **Measurable:** We will have reduced the number of steps involved in selling a home from fifty to twenty.
- **Attainable:** We will start by making our pricing model simpler and then gradually simplifying specific steps of the online experience, releasing these simplifications iteratively and obtaining customer feedback throughout.
- **Realistic:** Making online home-sale transactions simpler will enable the business to scale and improve profit margins per transaction.
- **Time related:** We will implement these simplifications within eight weeks and will have ten homes sold through this simplified approach within four weeks from release.

A few years ago, I worked with a large travel company that had several disparate product teams working on different solutions aimed at different customer segments. There was one team that catered exclusively to business travellers whilst another created products geared toward family holidays.

From talking to the product managers in the respective teams, it became apparent very quickly that each team did great work in creating features for their own customer groups. However, because each team acted as its own speedboat, they did

[158] George T. Doran, "There's a S.M.A.R.T. Way to Write Management's Goals and Objectives," *Management Review* 70, no. 11 (1981): 35–6.

not collaborate with other teams. As a result, the overall user experience was incoherent at best in places, and teams ended up duplicating huge amounts of effort and time.

The then newly appointed chief product officer realised the value in bringing all the different product teams together. She flew everyone out for a big off-site. One of the ground rules for the off-site was that participants were allowed to mention their teams and specific focus areas only once, as part of the introductions. For the rest of the day, people were encouraged to think about common problem areas for all travel customers and to come up with an overarching vision. It was fascinating to observe people who had never spoken, let alone worked together before, discuss such problems as "All travellers struggle to quickly find the best flight for them" or "We need to make travelling cheaper and more accessible."

A few weeks after the off-site, the travel company bought into an overarching product vision and a single consolidated product road map. To this day, the company uses a goal-oriented road map, with the distributed product teams collaborating around shared business and product goals.

When defined and used properly, goals are great collaboration and communication tools. Product managers have an important role to play with regard to both creating and driving goals, and they can use goals when trying to influence others. In the remainder of this chapter, we will examine how to best influence without authority. However, I strongly believe that influencing starts with something that I got so horribly wrong in the bull in a china shop situation I described earlier: listening.

3. Active and Reflective Listening

The best way to explain what active listening means is to share an example of a pitfall I have fallen into on numerous occasions:

> **Speaker:** We have decided to do X, Y, and Z. This seems like the best approach because…
>
> **Me** [thinking]: Why did he or she decide X, Y and Z? That doesn't make *any* sense! What was he or she thinking?

Even though I might have had the intent to listen to the speaker, I missed the core of what the speaker had to say. Instead, I listened only to my own judgment or interpretation and completely ignored the "because" part of the speaker's statement. At its core, active listening means that you are listening for meaning and spending more time listening than speaking.

I learned a lot from reading *The Art of Active Listening* in which authors Josh Gibson and Fynn Walker explain how active listening requires you to understand, interpret, and evaluate what you're being told.[159] Active listening also means that you focus your *full* attention on the speaker. This means that whenever you feel an inner urge to say something—to respond—try to stop this urge and instead concentrate on what's being said.

In their book, Gibson and Walker stress the importance of listening actively:

- Active listening encourages people to open up.
- Active listening reduces the chance of misunderstandings.
- Active listening helps to resolve problems and conflicts.
- Active listening builds trust.

Active listening is the key to empathy and relationship building. I like Gibson and Walker's simple breakdown of human communication: "In simple terms, speaking is one person reaching out, and listening is another person accepting and taking hold. Together, they form communication, and this is the basis of all human relationships."

Let's go back to my personal confession at the start of this chapter, where I admitted to not listening. I came in with my set opinions and did not spend enough time observing and listening. Instead of figuring out why my new colleagues were doing things a certain way, or trying to truly listen, I made up my mind that my colleagues simply didn't know what they were doing.

After reading *The Art of Active Listening*, I have since learned about seven common barriers to active listening:

1. **Your ignorance and delusion:** The first barrier to active listening is simply not realising that you aren't. People can get by without developing their listening skills. I'm sure you've come across at least one person who felt that

---

[159] Fynn Walker and Josh Gibson, *The Art of Active Listening: How to Double Your Communication Skills in 30 Days* (Seattle: Amazon Digital Services, 2011); "Book Review: 'The Art of Active Listening,'" Marc Abraham, April 13, 2017, https://marcabraham.com/2017/04/13/book-review-the-art-of-active-listening/.

he or she was listening actively. In reality, this person merely allowed the other person to speak in his or her presence.

2. **Your reluctance:** When you actively listen to another person, it may be that you become involved in his or her situation in some way. There might be instances when you are reluctant to get involved and, as a result, fail to lend a sympathetic and understanding ear.

3. **Your bias and prejudice:** Your personal interpretation of what you're hearing may cause you to respond negatively to the speaker. You either assume that you know the situation because you've had a similar experience in the past or you allow your preconceptions to colour the way you respond.

4. **Your lack of interest:** You may simply not be interested in what the speaker is saying. We all know this can happen when you feel the conversation topic is uninspiring or when you feel that you've heard something before. As a result, you're dismissing what the other person is saying as irrelevant.

5. **Your opinion of the speaker:** Your opinion of the speaker as a person may influence the extent to which you are happy to pay attention and to give your time to the speaker. Often when you don't like the speaker, this is likely to influence your desire to listen to him or her. I've also noticed how in certain places the status of the speaker has a big influence on whether he or she is being listened to. In these places, the CEO tends to be listened to automatically, whereas "people of lower rank" might struggle to be heard.

6. **Your own feelings:** Your ability to listen to other people can easily be affected by how you're feeling at a particular moment. For example, if you're in a good mood, you might feel more inclined to listen actively and to offer your best advice based on what you've just heard. In contrast, if you're in a bad mood, the last thing you might want to do is listen to someone else's thoughts and to offer advice in response.

7. **The wrong time and place:** These are the physical factors that influence whether you are willing or able to actively listen to what you are being told. For example, having a heart-to-heart conversation in a busy coffee shop is unlikely to positively influence your ability to listen actively.

Reflecting on the period when I struggled to listen to others, I clearly suffered from the third and fourth barriers: my bias and prejudice combined with an overall lack of interest. To address these barriers, I read about the four components of active listening:

1. **Acceptance:** Acceptance is about respecting the person you're talking to regardless of what the other person has to say but purely because you're

talking to another human being. Accepting means trying to avoid expressing agreement or disagreement with what the other person is saying, at least initially. I've often made this mistake—being too keen to express my views and thus encouraging the speaker to take a very defensive stance in the conversation.

2. **Honesty:** Honesty comes down to being open about your reactions to what you've heard. Similar to the acceptance component, honest reactions given too soon can easily stifle further explanation on the part of the speaker. I want to stress here that an honest reaction can be both verbal and nonverbal. Therefore, keep your facial expression in check if you don't want to give an honest reaction too early!

3. **Empathy:** Empathy is about your ability to understand the speaker's situation on an emotional level, based on your own view. Basing your understanding on your own view instead of on a sense of what should be felt creates empathy instead of sympathy. Empathy can also be defined as your desire to feel the speaker's emotions, regardless of your own experience.

4. **Specifics:** Specifics refers to the need to deal in details rather than in generalities. For communication to be worthwhile, you should ask the speaker to be more specific, encouraging the speaker to open up more or own the problem he or she is trying to raise.

Respecting and empathising with the person I was talking to were the two main things that I started putting into practice in order to become an active listener. Similarly, I have met people who started improving their listening skills by making more eye contact with others or avoiding what I call "me too" stories.

In *The Art of Active Listening,* Gibson and Walker provide several practical pointers on how to best create or improve active listening skills:

1. Minimise external distractions.
2. Face the speaker.
3. Maintain eye contact.
4. Focus on the speaker.
5. Be open-minded.
6. Be sincerely interested.
7. Have sympathy and feel empathy.
8. Assess the emotion, not just the words.
9. Respond appropriately.
10. Minimise internal distractions.
11. Avoid "me" stories.

12. Don't be scared of silence.
13. Take notes.
14. Practice emotional intelligence.
15. Check your understanding.

Once you have listened actively, reflective listening is a useful technique you can apply next. Reflective listening is concerned with how you process what you have heard.[160] This doesn't mean that you should simply repeat or parrot what the other person has just told you.[161] In contrast, you endeavour to imagine what it would be like to be in the same situation as or frame of mind of the person speaking. Reflective listening is all about displaying genuine empathy for the other person. Instead of simply mirroring what he or she just mentioned, you apply the following two steps:

1. Seek to fully understand the speaker's idea or thought.
2. Offer the idea back to the speaker to check that you have understood it correctly.

Again, this doesn't mean that you have to automatically agree with what the speaker has said. Too often, I have seen well-meaning people veer to the other end of the active listening spectrum. For example:

Speaker: Charging the customer extra for this new service is a bad idea.

Listener: Uh-huh [nods].

Speaker: I just can't see us making any money out of this new service.

Listener: Yeah, you're saying that you can't see us making any money out of this new service.

Speaker: Cool. I'm pleased that you agree with me on not charging for this new service.

---

[160] Carl R. Rogers, "A Theory of Therapy, Personality, and Interpersonal Relationships, as Developed in the Client-Centered Framework," in *Psychology: A Study of a Science*, Vol. 3, Formulations of the Person and the Social Context (New York: McGraw-Hill, 1959), 184–256.
[161] Kyle Arnold, "Behind the Mirror: Reflective Listening and Its Tain in the Work of Carl Rogers," *The Humanistic Psychologist* 42 (2014): 354–69.

Instead, reflective listening is about truly trying to understand what the speaker is saying and why. As a reflective listener, you make every effort to understand where the other speaker is coming from:

> **Speaker:** Charging the customer extra for this new service is a bad idea.
>
> **Listener:** Just to make sure I understand you correctly, you're saying that we shouldn't charge extra for this service. Is that correct?
>
> **Speaker:** Yes, that is correct.
>
> **Listener:** Why do you feel that we shouldn't charge for this new service? I can imagine this might be because you don't believe in the additional value of this service or that you think the customer is paying a large amount as it is. Am I thinking along the right lines?
>
> **Speaker:** Yes. My main concern is that we end up losing customers if we increase prices.
>
> **Listener:** I see. Perhaps we can look at alternative pricing models. How would you feel about that?

This simple example shows how you can play back what you have heard without simply repeating what the other person has just said. In the next and final section of this chapter, we will look at how listening comes into play when influencing without authority or in tense situations.

4. Influencing without Authority or in Tense Situations

At the beginning of this book, I described the multifaceted role of the product manager. You may recall the positioning of the product manager at the intersection of user experience, business, and technology. It is this intersection that I want to end at because it is how you influence from this position that determines how effectively you manage people and, as a result, the success of your product.

As I confessed at the beginning of this chapter, I upset numerous people when starting a new product management role by not picking my battles. Consequently, I acted like a bull in a china shop and upset quite a few people in the process.

I would almost go as far as saying that as a product manager, you can't afford to alienate too many people. Let's be clear: this doesn't mean that each and every colleague needs to be your best friend. Quite the opposite: a good product person knows how to challenge constructively.

However, looking back on the early years of my product management career, I now realise that product management is as much about paying respect to the people you work with as it is to the products you work on. More specifically, I realised how much product managers need to build relationships with colleagues *because* of the very nature of product management: we need to manage a lot of different people without having authority over any of them.

You might be reading this and thinking back to a sense of frustration I have heard many product managers talk about: being accountable for delivering value without having any authority over the people critical to delivering the value. Whether it is internal stakeholders, customers, developers, or designers, there is only so much we can do as product people to influence and develop the level of buy-in and cooperation required to create successful products. There's no reason to despair, though; we can influence without authority.

Figure 6.2. Summary of the Cohen-Bradford model of influencing without authority[162]

---

[162] Allan R. Cohen and David L. Bradford, *Influence without Authority*, 2nd Ed. (New York: Wiley, 1991).

Reading *Influence without Authority* by Allan R. Cohen and David L. Bradford was a real eye-opener.[163] In this book, the authors describe ways to influence people and situations when you do not have authority over others. The book is underpinned by the eponymous model developed by Cohen and Bradford. (See fig. 6.2.)

Influence without Authority offers three key principles that will benefit product managers in getting the most out of other people or when managing tense situations: (1) currencies of exchange, (2) gaining clarity on your objectives, and (3) deciding with whom to attempt exchanges:[164]

1. **The currencies of exchange:** The Cohen-Bradford model is based on exchange and reciprocity—making trades for what you desire in return for what the other person desires. For example, when working with developers, I used to ask, "Can you implement this new feature?" Often he or she would respond with a simple no or say, "It's too difficult." In return, I would then repeat the request, but the other person's response would remain unchanged. This uncomfortable dance would continue for a while until one of us decided to give in. I have since come to realise that thinking about the other person's "currencies" makes it much easier to navigate these situations and to take the tension out of them. There are several potential currencies that one can use to trade, which I'll discuss in the next section.

2. **Gaining clarity on your objectives:** For the Cohen-Bradford model to work effectively, it's important that you figure out exactly what you want and prioritise your goals accordingly. Earlier in this chapter, we looked at goal setting and how to use shared goals as a collaboration tool. Communicating clear goals usually makes it much easier for others to see the bigger picture.[165]

3. **Deciding with whom to attempt exchanges:** The ability to consider and decide potential allies to exchange is a critical part of the Cohen-Bradford model, and their book outlines some valuable considerations for how to exchange directly with a potential ally. Going back to my mistakes made around picking battles and choosing allies, I now realise the value in

---

[163] "Book Review: 'Influence without Authority,'" Marc Abraham, April 25, 2017, https://marcabraham.com/2017/04/25/book-review-influence-without-authority/.

[164] Allan and Bradford, *Influence without Authority*, 36–51.

[165] Liyin Jin, Szu-chi Huang, and Ying Zhang, "The Unexpected Positive Impact of Fixed Structures on Goal Completion," *Journal of Consumer Research* 40, no. 4 (2013): 711–25; "5 Strategies for Big-Picture Thinking," Justin Rosenstein, Fast Company, September 25, 2014, https://www.fastcompany.com/3036143/5-strategies-for-big-picture-thinking.

stepping back to identify potential allies and how best to build a relationship with them.

Inspiration-Related Currencies

Inspiration-related currencies reflect inspirational goals that provide meaning to the work a person does:

- **Vision:** You can help overcome personal objections if you can inspire the potential ally to see the larger significance of your request, describing the bigger picture.
- **Excellence:** The opportunity to do something important really well and with genuine excellence can be highly motivating.
- **Moral/ethical correctness:** Most organisational members would like to act according to what they perceive to be the ethical, moral, or correct thing to do.

Task-Related Currencies

Task-related currencies are directly related to getting the job done. They relate to a person's ability to perform his or her assigned tasks or to the satisfactions that arise from accomplishment.

- **New resources:** Such resources as budget, people, space, equipment, or time are important currencies when it comes to enabling someone to get the job done.
- **Challenge:** The chance to work at tasks that provide a challenge or stretch is one of the most widely valued currencies in modern organisational life.
- **Assistance:** Although large numbers of people desire increased responsibilities and challenge, most have tasks they need help on or would be glad to shed.
- **Organisational support:** This currency is most valued by someone who is working on a project and needs public backing or behind-the-scenes help in selling the project to others.
- **Rapid response:** It can be worth a great deal for a colleague or boss to know that you will respond urgently to requests.
- **Information:** Recognising that knowledge is power, some people value any information that may help them shape the performance of their unit.

Position-Related Currencies

These currencies enhance a person's position in the organisation and thereby indirectly aid the person's ability to accomplish tasks or advance a career.

- **Recognition:** Many people gladly will extend themselves for a project when they believe their contributions will be recognised, so it's important to spread recognition around and recognise the right people.
- **Visibility to higher-ups:** Ambitious employees realise that, in a large organisation, opportunities to perform for or be recognised by powerful people can be a deciding factor in achieving future opportunities, information, or promotions.
- **Reputation:** Reputation is another variation on recognition. A good reputation can pave the way for a variety of opportunities, whilst a bad one can quickly shut the person out and make it difficult to perform.
- **Insiderness**: For some members, being in the inner circle is the most valued currency. One sign of this currency is having insider information, and another is being connected to important people.
- **Importance:** A variation on the currency of insider knowledge and contacts is the chance to feel important. Inclusion and information are symbols of that, but just being acknowledged as an important player counts for the large number of people who feel their value is underrecognised.
- **Contacts:** Related to many of the previous currencies is the opportunity for making contacts, which creates a network of people who can be approached when needed for mutually helpful transactions.

Relationship-Related Currencies

Relationship-related currencies are more connected to strengthening the relationship with someone than directly accomplishing the organisation's tasks.

- **Acceptance/inclusion:** Some people most value the feeling that they are close to others, whether an individual or a group/department. They are receptive to those who offer warmth and liking as currencies.
- **Understanding/listening/sympathy:** Colleagues who feel beleaguered by the demands of the organisation, isolation, or unsupported by the boss place an especially high value on a sympathetic ear.
- **Personal support:** For some people, at particular times, having the support of others is the currency they value most. When a colleague is feeling stressed, upset, vulnerable, or needy, he or she will doubly appreciate—and remember—a thoughtful gesture.

Personal Currencies

These currencies could form an infinite list of idiosyncratic needs. They are valued because they enhance the individual's sense of self. They may be derived from task or interpersonal activity.

- **Gratitude:** Although gratitude may be another form of recognition or support, it is not necessarily a job-related one that can be valued highly by some people who make a point of being helpful to others. For their efforts, some people want appreciation from the receiver, expressed in thanks or deference.
- **Ownership/involvement:** Another currency often valued by organisational members is the chance to feel that they are partly in control of something important or have a chance to make a major contribution.
- **Self-concept:** This currency covers those that are consistent with a person's image of himself or herself.
- **Comfort:** Some people place high value on personal comfort. Lovers of routine and haters of risk, they will do almost anything to avoid being hassled or embarrassed.

Negative Currencies

Currencies are what people value. But it is also possible to think of negative currencies, things that people do not value and wish to avoid. Think of negative currencies as the stick to punish someone with, either by withholding payments or by displaying behaviour that is directly undesirable.

Withholding payments

- Not giving recognition
- Not offering support
- Not providing challenge
- Threatening to quit the situation

Directly undesirable

- Raising your voice, yelling
- Refusing to cooperate when asked
- Escalating the issue upward to a common boss

- Going public with the issue, making lack of cooperation visible
- Attacking a person's reputation or integrity

Gain clarity on your objectives:[166]

- What are your primary goals?
- What personal factors get in the way?
- Be flexible about achieving your goals.
- Adjust the expectation of your role and your ally's role.

Decide with whom to attempt exchanges:[167]

- **Centrality of the ally:** How powerful is the other person? Power means more than hierarchical position: What needed resources does he or she control? How exclusive is the person's control of those resources? How dependent are you on that person for success?
- **Amount of effort/credits needed:** Do you already have a relationship with the person, or will you be starting from scratch? Is the person likely to insist on trading in currencies you do not command or cannot gain access to? Will the person be satisfied as long as you at least pay your respects and stay in touch, without asking anything directly?
- **Alternatives available:** Do you know anyone whose support will help gain the support of the potential ally? In other words, who can influence the ally if you are not able to directly? If you can't influence the person in the right direction, can you find a way to neutralise him or her? Can you reshape your project to take the person's opposition into account or to skirt the person's worst concern?

In conclusion, being able to influence without authority is an essential skill for any product manager, whether you are junior or senior. Having reflected on my previous behaviours, I now see how critical such soft skills as being able to influence are to being an effective product manager.

Key Takeaways

I remember starting my product management career being quite sniffy about the people aspect of product management. Acting like a bull in a china shop and

---

[166] Cohen and Bradford, *Influence without Authority*, 82.
[167] Ibid., 134–36.

learning some confrontational insights have taught me that managing people is an important factor in a product's success.

1. **Use a shared vision and goals to get people on board.** Providing direction is a prime responsibility of any product manager. A product vision that people buy into, as well as shared goals, will help make your chosen direction more tangible.
2. **Pick your battles, especially with difficult stakeholders.** The fact that not all your colleagues have to become your close friends does not mean that they should all become your enemies. Picking your battles is key when you are looking to achieve certain goals and when you are dependent on others to achieve those goals. If you feel that picking battles sounds too much like a war metaphor, then think of it as influencing without authority in order to achieve specific results.
3. **Don't talk, just listen.** Empathy is a critical (soft) skill for any product manager. To get started with developing more empathy, start by truly listening. Active listening involves so much more than just keeping your ears open; assessing the emotion, not just the words, and minimising internal distractions are key if you want to really listen to what someone else is saying.

How to Apply These Takeaways

- **Start with goals.** Whether you have just joined a new organisation or have just started working on a product, you can use goals to set the tone and give yourself and others a shareable direction to work toward. Especially given the wide range of stakeholders you are likely to work with, having shared goals will make subsequent conversations and decision making a lot easier.
- **Facilitate a good kick-off session.** Use a kick-off session to start working on a product to convey the goals you are looking to achieve and to explain the context around these goals. This will stimulate a healthy discussion about the *what* and the *why* of the proposed goals before you decide together on *how* you are going to achieve these goals.
- **Identify key stakeholders and build a relationship.** When you are clear on what you are looking to achieve and why, you can start mapping out who your key stakeholders are and how you are likely to need them to achieve your goals. For example, "I need Sally, the head of sales, to provide me with five customers who are happy to take part in beta testing of the product," or "Joe can sign off on the marketing budget we need to launch this product." Thinking up-front about who you need to influence or build a working

relationship with does not need to be some sort of Machiavellian exercise. Understanding who can help you achieve certain results will allow you to approach people in the right manner and use the right currencies to exchange with them.

Conclusion

I didn't think. I experimented.

—Anthony Burgess

"What are the key things I need to do in order to become a great product manager?" Emily asked me. She had been a product manager for several years and wanted to take the next step. "Is there a certification I can study for that would help me to stand out as a fully qualified product manager?"

Unfortunately, Emily seemed to be disappointed by my answer. I said, "There are many great courses and books out there that might be helpful to you, but I'm afraid there's not one silver bullet for product management."

There is no single holy grail when it comes to becoming an outstanding product manager or to creating a world-class product. There are, however, a wide array of tools and techniques that you can apply that will help you build products customers love. I have learned almost all the methods and suggestions mentioned in this book by stumbling across them and figuring out by trial by error which are the ones that work. My hope is that you will find value in using this book as a true toolkit, applying its content as and when you see fit. Don't worry if a certain technique does not pan out as expected the first, or even the second or third, time around. In my experience, the key to good product management and creating awesome products is trying, learning, and trying again.

I would be very grateful for your thoughts after reading this book. Good or bad, your input will help me learn and iterate. Please check marcabraham.com or drop me a line at myproductmanagementtoolkit@gmail.com. Thank you!

Acknowledgments

I would like to thank several people for their support of this book and their varied contributions to its creation. Jo Wickremasinghe, Philip Brook, and Toon Gerbrands for acting as sounding boards when I was toying with the idea. Craig Strong, Roman Pichler, Lonnie Rosenbaum, and Simon Whatley for reviewing my draft chapters and providing valuable feedback. Rachel Smith for creating great illustrations and "getting" what I was trying to achieve.

My biggest thanks goes to my wife, Tracy Abraham, for her unconditional support and for going along with yet another one of my wild ideas!

About the Author

Marc Abraham is an experienced product management practitioner who has worked for a large number of successful digital organisations and is part of the team behind Mind the Product, an international product community of more than one hundred thousand members. Having begun his professional career as a corporate lawyer, Marc took up blogging at marcabraham.com as a way of discovering more about the digital ecosystem and ultimately as a way of breaking into it. He writes and speaks about his lessons learned, encouraging product managers to retain curiosity and pursue a journey of continuous learning.

Marc lives in London with his wife and two children.

Made in the USA
Coppell, TX
23 June 2021